FIRST 50 SONGS
YOU SHOULD STRUM ON THE GUITAR

ISBN 978-1-4950-3056-7

HAL•LEONARD®
CORPORATION

7777 W. BLUEMOUND RD. P.O. BOX 13819 MILWAUKEE, WI 53213

Visit Hal Leonard Online at
www.halleonard.com

The A Team

Words and Music by Ed Sheeran

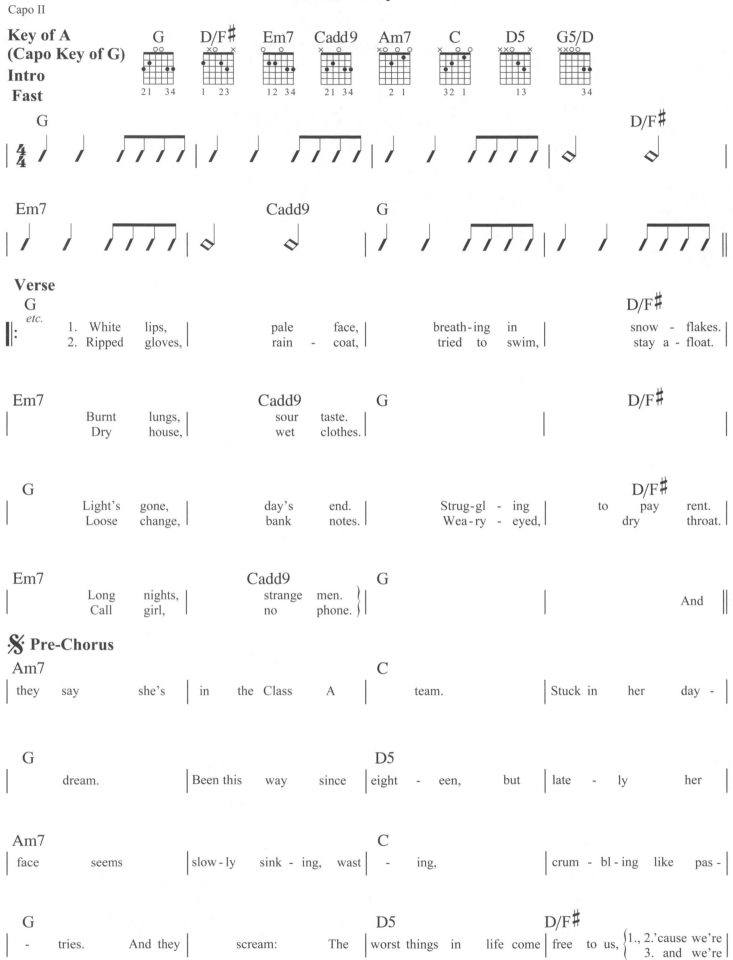

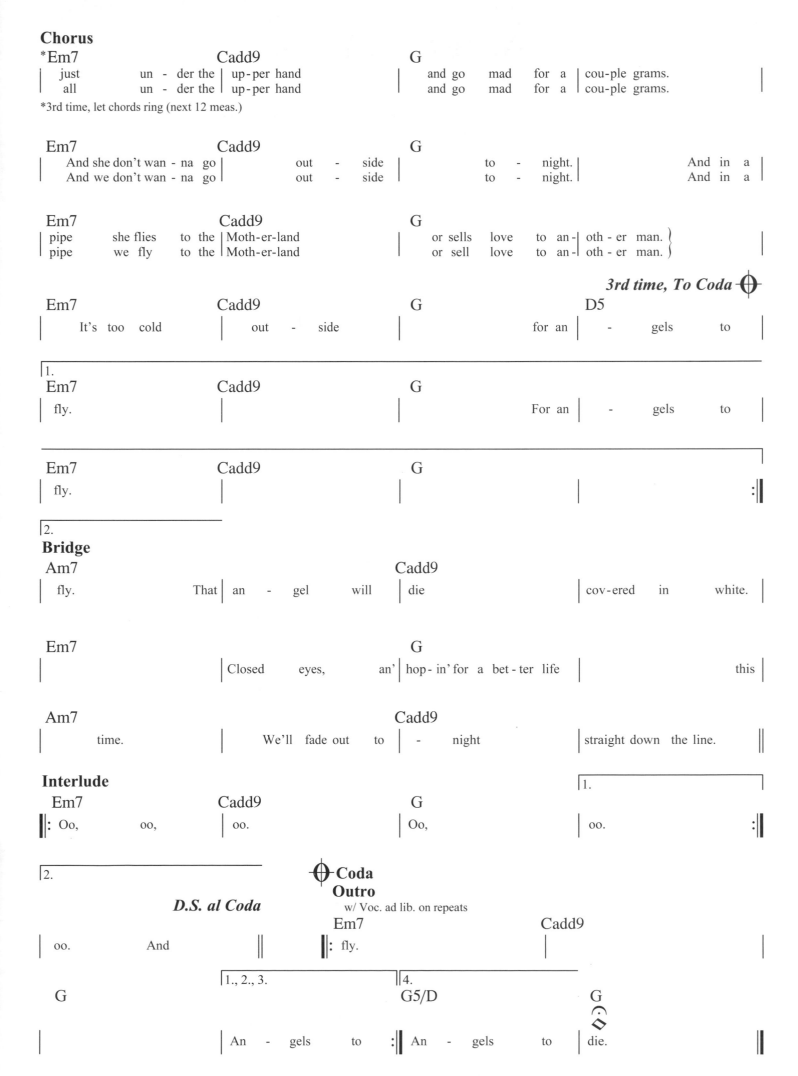

American Pie

Words and Music by Don McLean

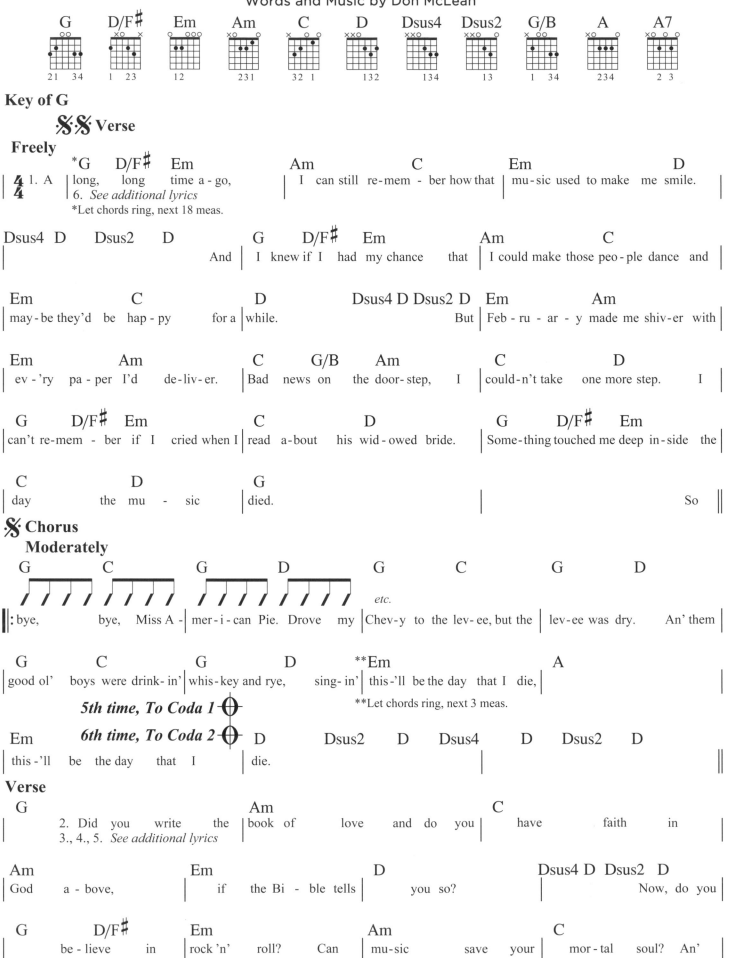

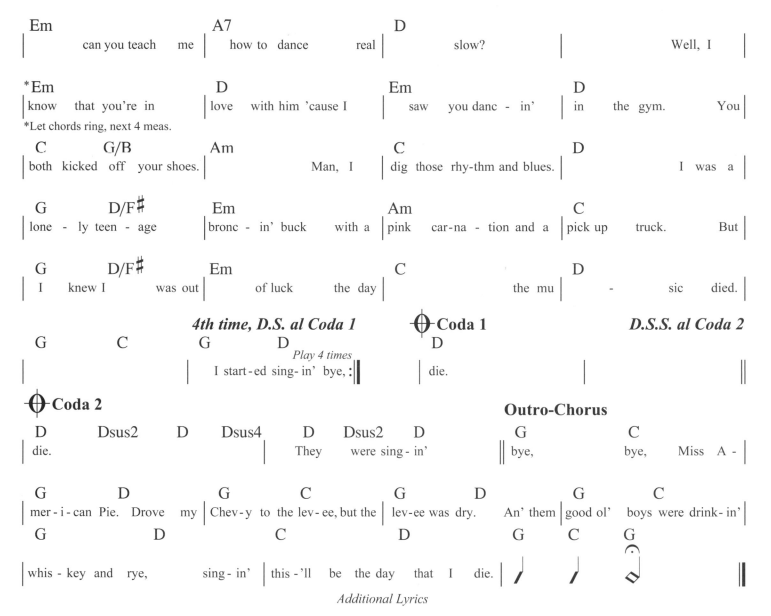

Additional Lyrics

3. Now, for ten years we've been on our own,
And moss grows fat on a rollin' stone.
But that's not how it used to be
When the jester sang for the king and queen
In a coat he borrowed from James Dean
And a voice that came from you and me.
Oh, and while the king was looking down,
The jester stole his thorny crown.
The courtroom was adjourned;
No verdict was returned.
And while Lenin read a book on Marx,
The quartet practiced in the park,
And we sang dirges in the dark the day the music died.
We were singin'…

4. Helter-skelter in a summer swelter,
The birds flew off with a fallout shelter,
Eight miles high and fallin' fast.
It landed foul on the grass.
The players tried a forward pass
With the jester on the sidelines in a cast.
Now the half-time air was sweet perfume
While the sergeants played a marching tune,
We all got up to dance,
Oh, but we never got the chance
'Cause the players tried to take the field;
The marching band refused to yield.
Do you recall what was revealed the day the music died?
We started singin'…

5. Oh, and there we were all in one place,
A generation lost in space
With no time left to start again.
So come on, Jack be nimble, Jack be quick,
Jack flash sat on a candlestick
'Cause fire is the devil's only friend.
Oh, and as I watched him on the stage,
My hands were clenched in fists of rage.
No angel born in hell
Could break that Satan's spell.
And as the flames climbed high into the night
To light the sacrificial rite,
I saw Satan laughing with delight the day the music died.
He was singin'…

6. I met a girl who sang the blues
And I asked her for some happy news
But she just smiled and turned away.
I went down to the sacred store
Where I'd heard the music years before
But the man there said the music wouldn't play.
And in the streets the children screamed,
The lovers cried an' the poets dreamed.
But not a word was spoken;
The church bells all were broken.
An' the three men I admire most,
The Father, Son and the Holy Ghost,
They caught the last train for the coast the day the music died.
An' they were singin'…

Baby, I Love Your Way

Words and Music by Peter Frampton

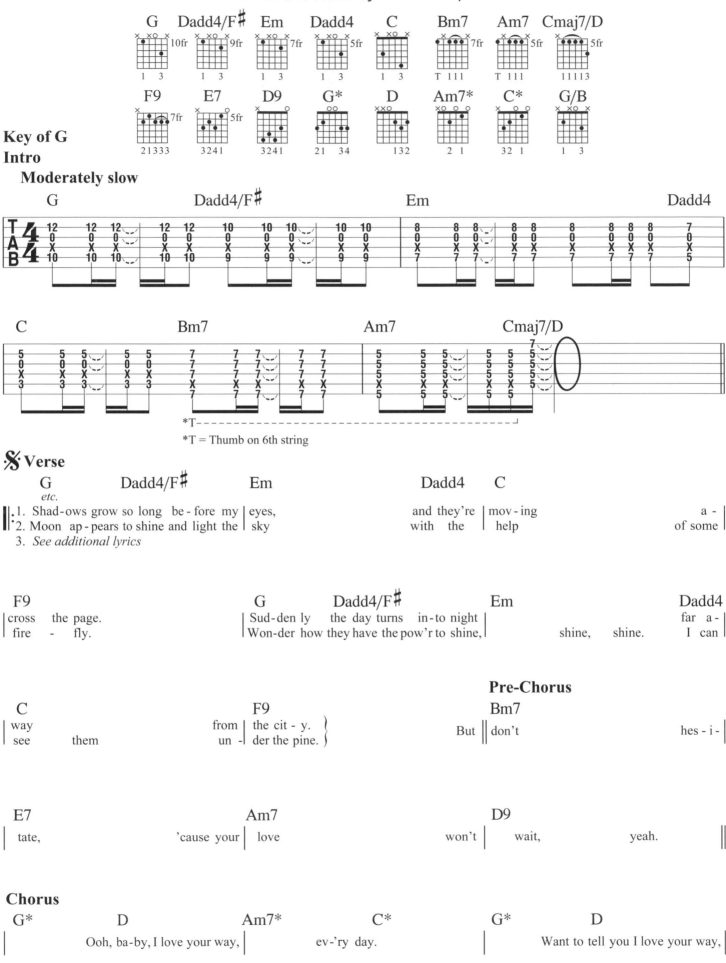

Key of G

Intro

Moderately slow

*T = Thumb on 6th string

Verse

G   Dadd4/F#   Em   Dadd4   C

etc.

1. Shad-ows grow so long be-fore my | eyes,   and they're | mov-ing   a -
2. Moon ap-pears to shine and light the | sky   with the | help   of some

3. *See additional lyrics*

F9   G   Dadd4/F#   Em   Dadd4

cross   the page. | Sud-den ly   the day turns   in-to night | far a -
fire - fly. | Won-der how they have the pow'r to shine,   shine,   shine.   I can

Pre-Chorus

C   F9   Bm7

way   from | the cit - y. | But || don't   hes - i -
see   them   un -| der the pine.

E7   Am7   D9

tate,   'cause your | love   won't   wait,   yeah.

Chorus

G*   D   Am7*   C*   G*   D

Ooh, ba-by, I love your way, | ev-'ry day. | Want to tell you I love your way,

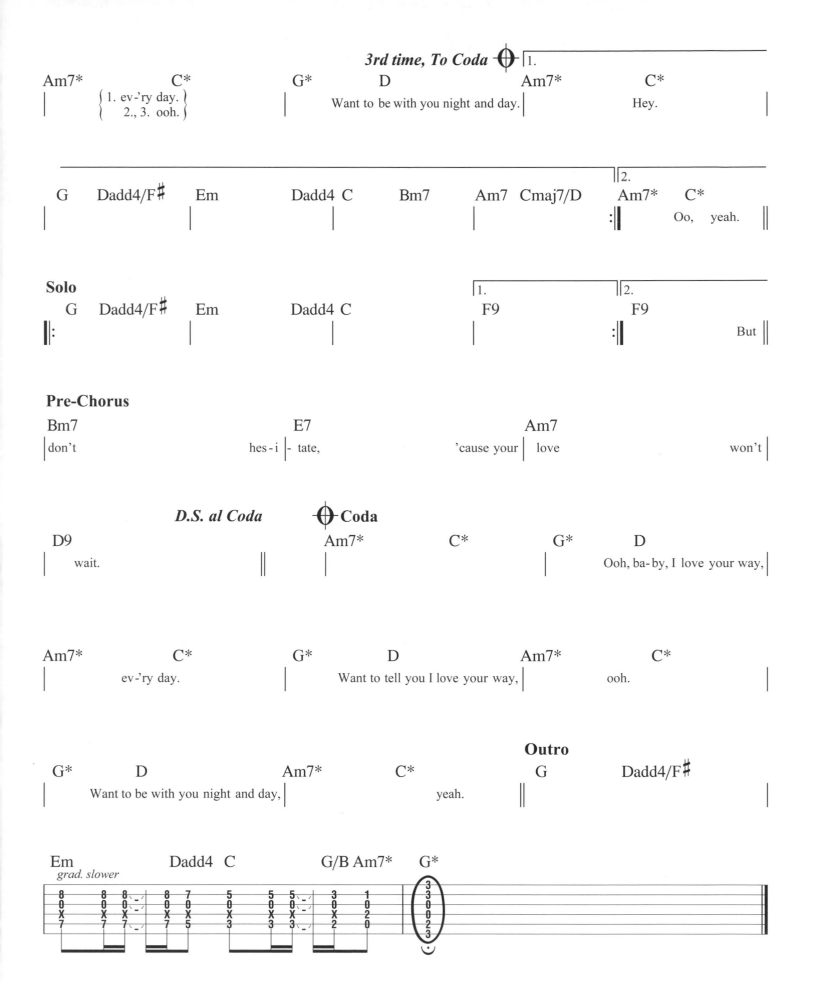

Additional Lyrics

3. I can see the sunset in your eyes,
   Brown and grey and blue besides.
   Clouds are stalking island in the sun.
   Wish I could buy one out of season.

Bad Moon Rising

Words and Music by John Fogerty

Key of D
Intro
Fast

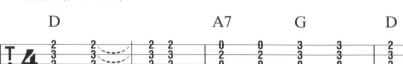

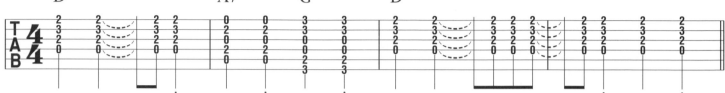

𝄋 Verse

D   A7   G   D

etc.
1. I   see   a | bad   moon   ris | - in'.
2. I   hear | hur - ri-canes   a blow | - in'.
3. *See additional lyrics*

D   A7   G   D

I   see | trou-ble   on   the way. |
I   know   the end | is   com-in'   soon. |

D   A7   G   D

I   see | earth - quakes   and light | - nin'.
I   fear | riv-ers   o - ver-flow | - in'.

D   A7   G   D

I   see | bad   times   to-day. |
I   hear   the voice | of rage   and ru | - in'.

Chorus

G   D

| Don't   go   a-round   to-night. | Well, it's | bound   to take   your   life. |

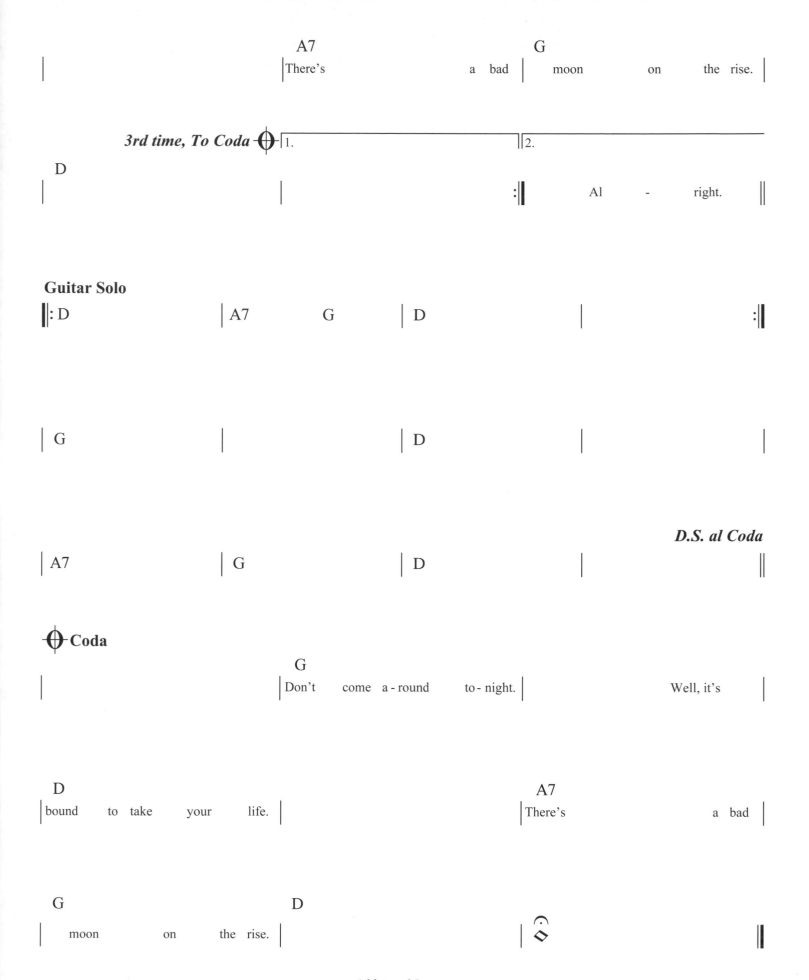

Better Together

Words and Music by Jack Johnson

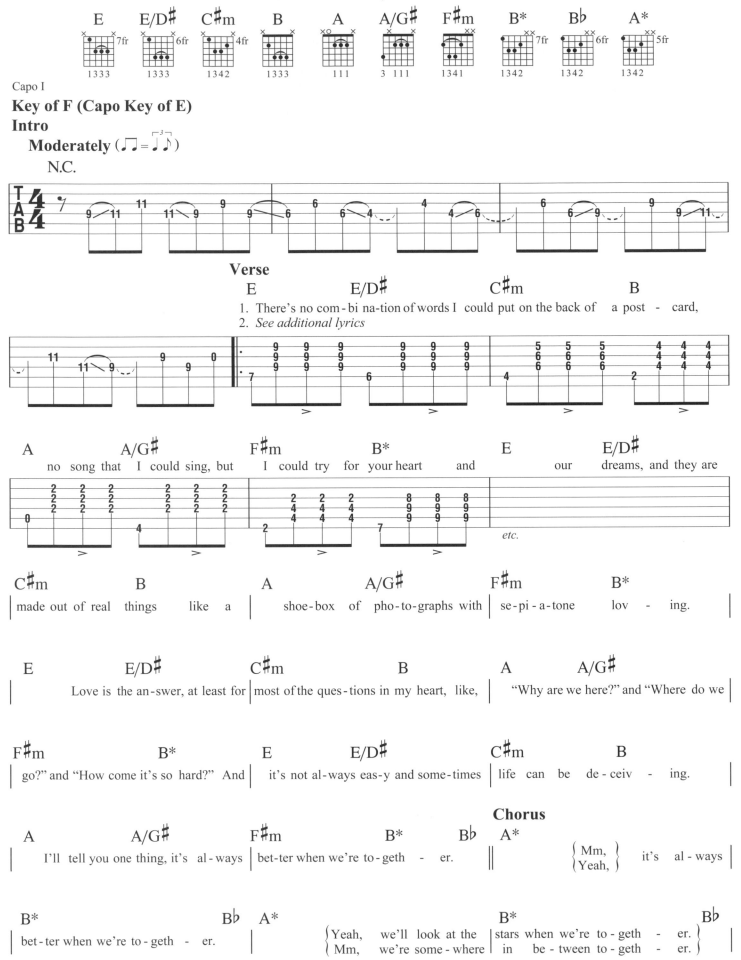

A* | B* | Bb A* | B* |

Well, it's al-ways | bet-ter when we're to-geth-er. | Yeah, it's al-ways | bet-ter when we're to-geth-er. ‖

Interlude

| E E/D# | C#m B | A A/G# | F#m B* | E E/D# |

C#m B | A A/G# | 1. F#m B* ‖ 2. F#m B* ‖

2. And all of these :‖

Bridge

F#m | B* | F#m | B* |

I be-lieve in mem-o-ries; they look so, | so pret-ty when I | sleep. Hey, now and, |

F#m | B* | F#m | B* |

and when I wake | up, you look so | pret-ty, sleep-ing next to | me. But there is |

A* | B* | A* | B* |

not e-nough | time. And there is no, | no song I could | sing. And there is no |

A* | B* | A* | B* |

com-bi-na-tion of | words I could say, but I will | still tell you one | thing: We're bet-ter to-geth-er. ‖

Outro

*E E/D# C#m B A A/G#

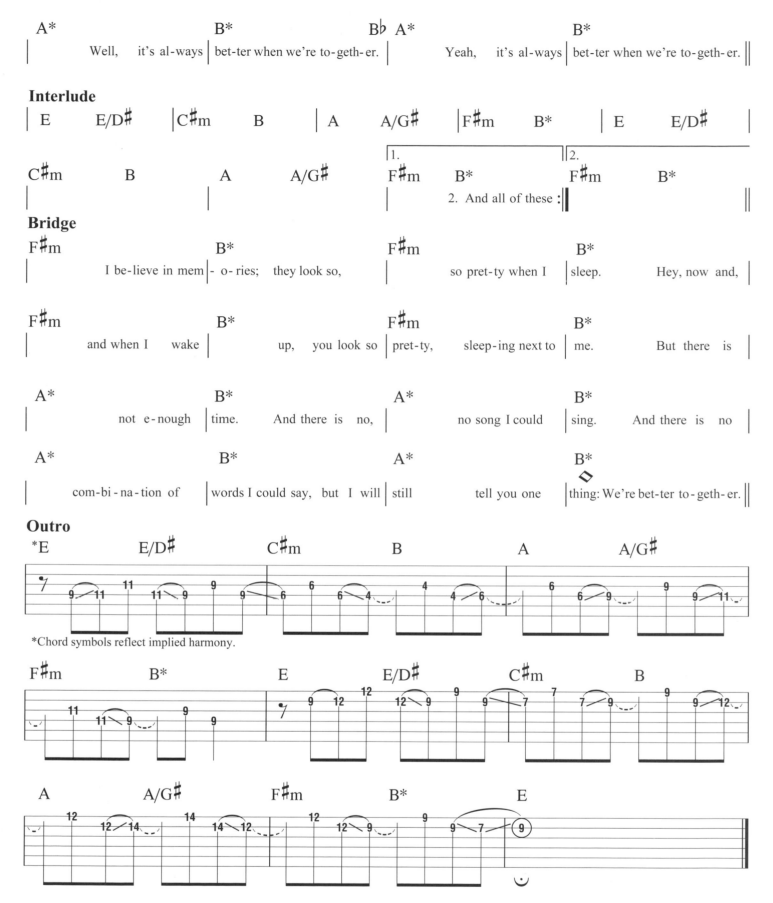

*Chord symbols reflect implied harmony.

F#m B* E E/D# C#m B

A A/G# F#m B* E

Additional Lyrics

2. And all of these moments just might find their way into my dreams tonight,
But I know that they'll be gone when the morning light sings or brings new things.
For tomorrow night you see
That they'll be gone too, too many things I have to do.
But if all of these dreams might find their way into my day-to-day scene,
I'd be under the impression I was somewhere in between
With only two, just me and you, not so many things we got to do
Or places we got to be. We'll sit beneath the mango tree now.

Blowin' in the Wind

Words and Music by Bob Dylan

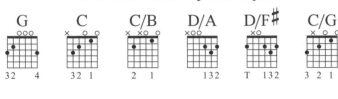

Capo VII

Key of D (Capo Key of G)

Intro

Verse

Moderately slow, in 2

1. How   man - y
2. How   man - y
3. *See additional lyrics*

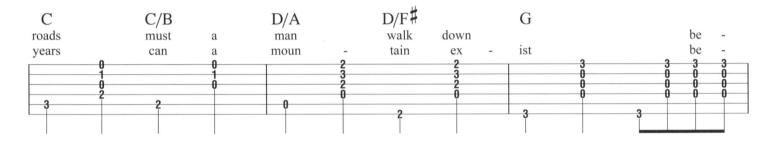

| roads | must | a | man | walk | down | | be - |
| years | can | a | moun | - tain | ex - ist | | be - |

etc.				
fore	you	call	him	a	man?
fore	it's	washed	him	to	the	sea?

Yes, 'n'   how   man - y   seas   must   a
Yes, 'n'   how   man - y   years   can   some

white   dove   sail   be -   fore   she
peo   -   ple   ex -   ist   be -   fore   they're   al -

sleeps   in   the   sand?   Yes, 'n'
lowed   to   be   free?   Yes, 'n'

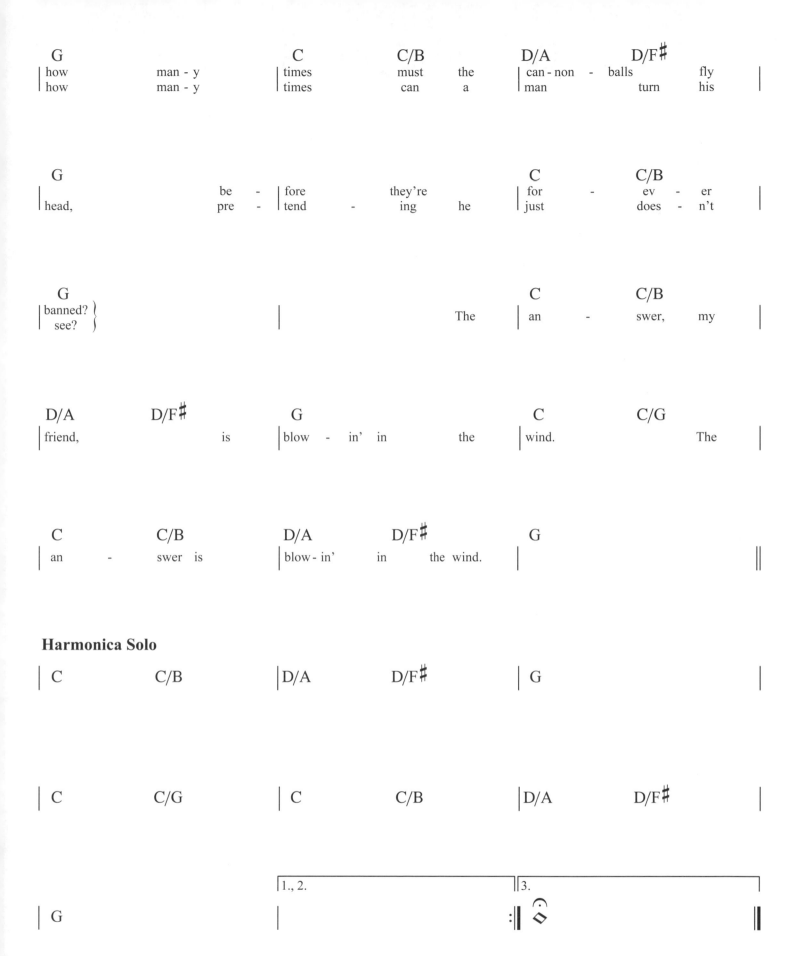

Harmonica Solo

Additional Lyrics

3. How many times must a man look up before he can see the sky?
   Yes, 'n' how many ears must one man have before he can hear people cry?
   Yes, 'n' how many deaths will it take till he knows that too many people have died?
   The answer, my friend, is blowin' in the wind.
   The answer is blowin' in the wind.

Brown Eyed Girl

Words and Music by Van Morrison

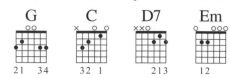

Key of G

Intro

Moderately fast

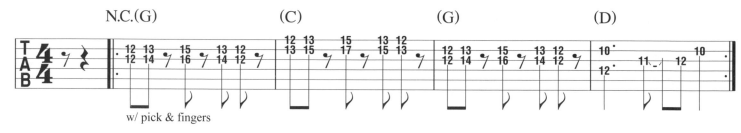

w/ pick & fingers

𝄋 Verse

G   C   G

1. Hey, where did we | go | days   when the rains
2. Now, what-ev-er hap | -pened | to Tues - day and so
3. *See additional lyrics*

D7   G   C

came?   Down   in the hol | -low,
slow?   Go - ing down   the old | mine   with a

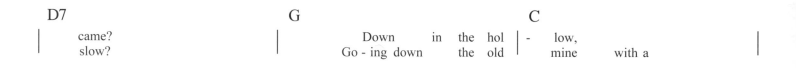

G   D7   G

play- in' a new | game.   Laugh-ing and a
tran - sis - tor ra | - di - o.   Stand-ing in the

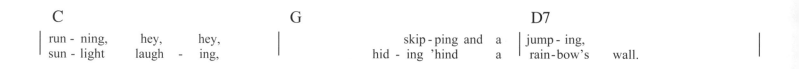

C   G   D7

run - ning,   hey,   hey, | skip - ping and a | jump - ing,
sun - light   laugh - ing, | hid - ing 'hind   a | rain-bow's   wall.

G   C   G

in the mis - ty morn | - ing   fog   with | our,   our
Slip - ping and a   slid | - ing | all a - long   the

14

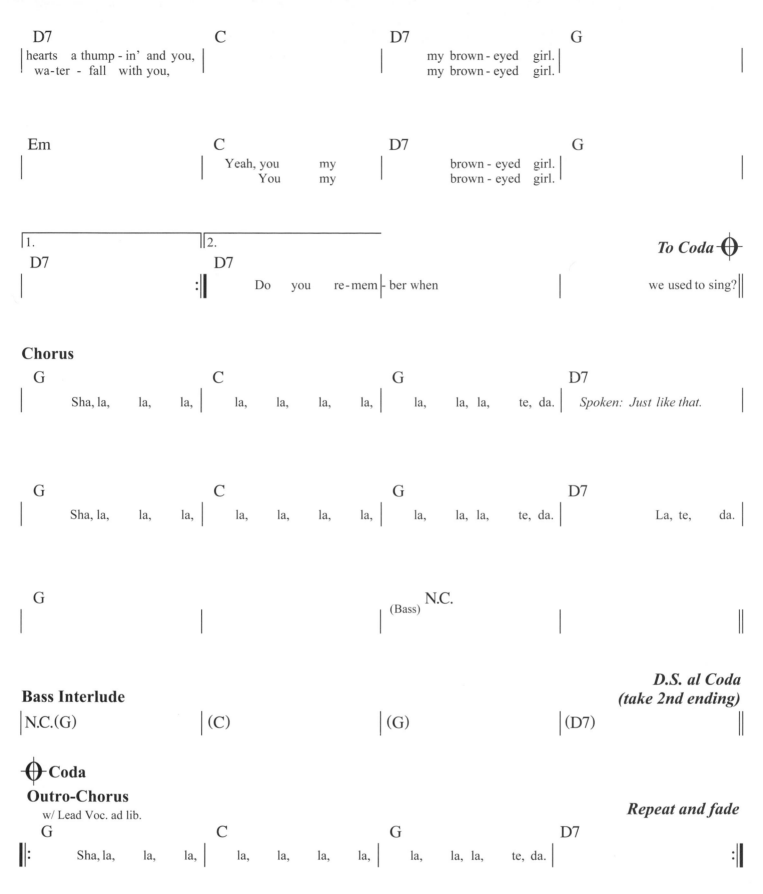

Chorus

Bass Interlude

⊕ Coda
Outro-Chorus

Additional Lyrics

3. So hard to find my way
   Now that I'm all on my own.
   I saw you just the other day;
   My, how you have grown.
   Cast my mem'ry back there, Lord.
   Sometimes I'm overcome thinkin' 'bout it.
   Making love in the green grass
   Behind the stadium with you,
   My brown-eyed girl.
   A, you my brown-eyed girl.

Building a Mystery

Words and Music by Sarah McLachlan and Pierre Marchand

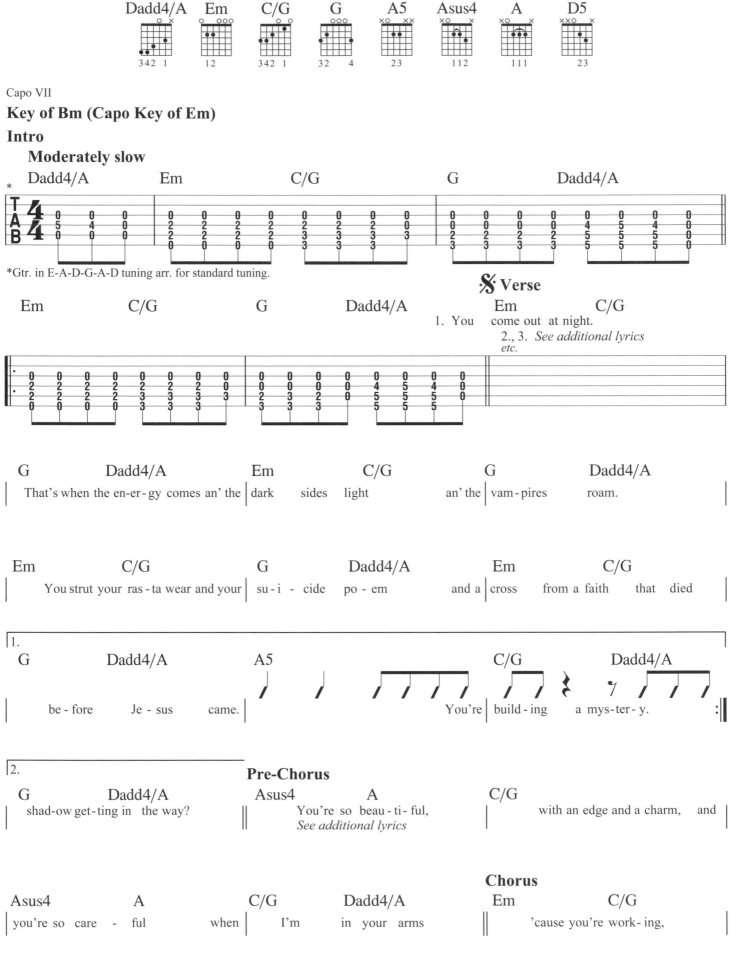

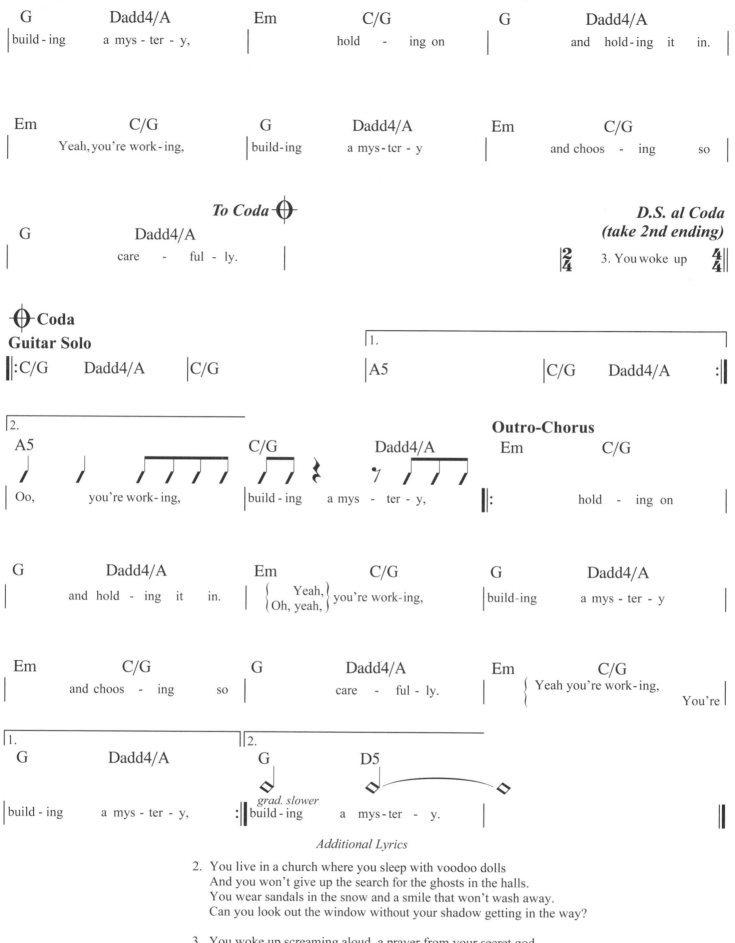

Additional Lyrics

2. You live in a church where you sleep with voodoo dolls
   And you won't give up the search for the ghosts in the halls.
   You wear sandals in the snow and a smile that won't wash away.
   Can you look out the window without your shadow getting in the way?

3. You woke up screaming aloud, a prayer from your secret god,
   To feed off of fears and hold back your tears, oh.
   You give us a tantrum and know-it-all grin
   Just when we need one, when the evening's thin.

Pre-Chorus You're a beautiful, a beautiful fucked up man.
   You're setting up your razor wire shrine...

Chasing Cars

Words and Music by Gary Lightbody, Tom Simpson,
Paul Wilson, Jonathan Quinn and Nathan Connolly

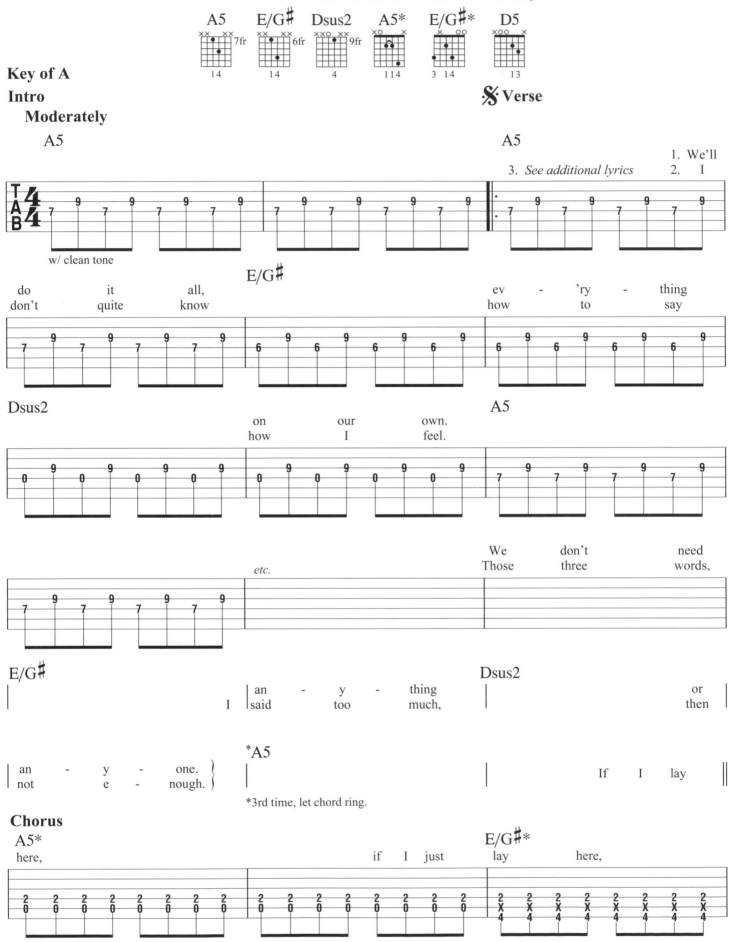

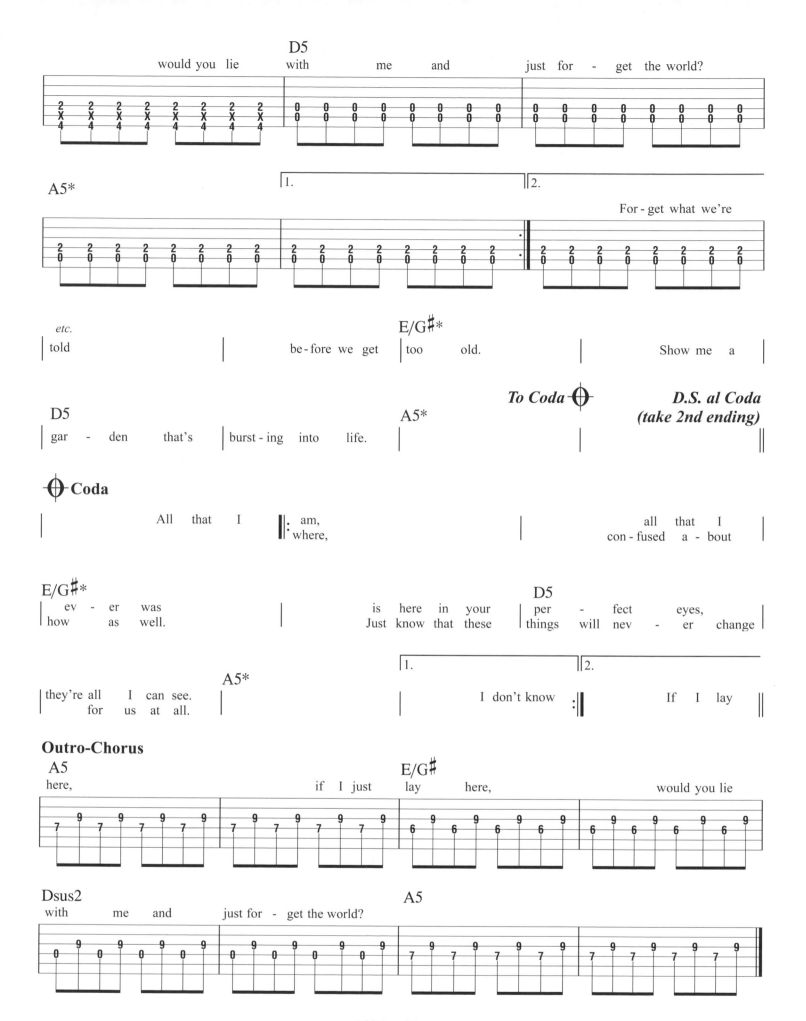

Daughter

Words and Music by Stone Gossard, Jeffrey Ament,
Eddie Vedder, Michael McCready and David Abbruzzese

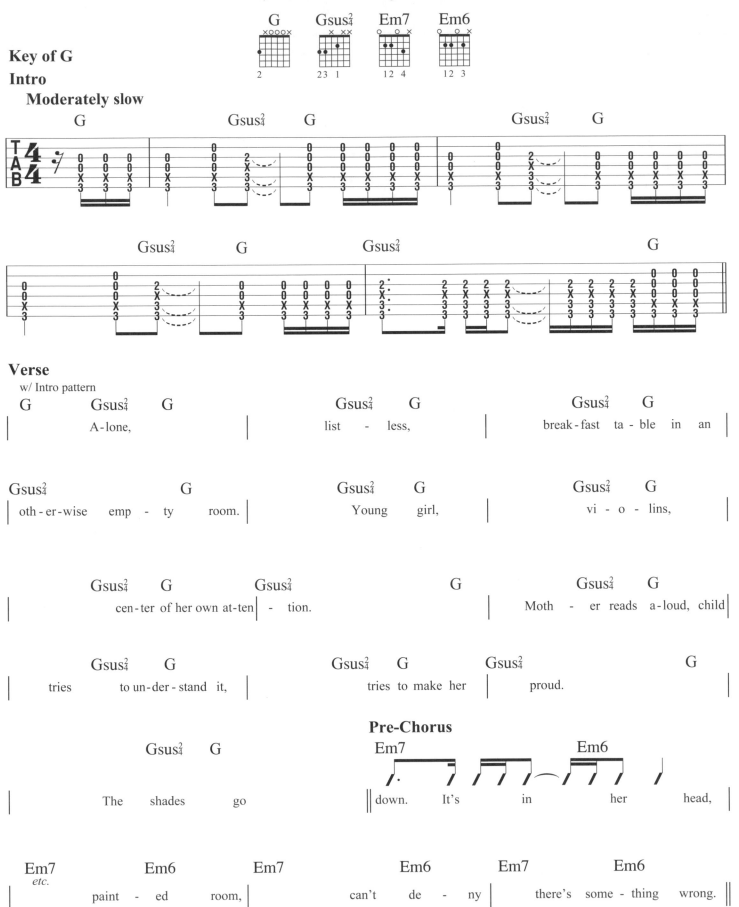

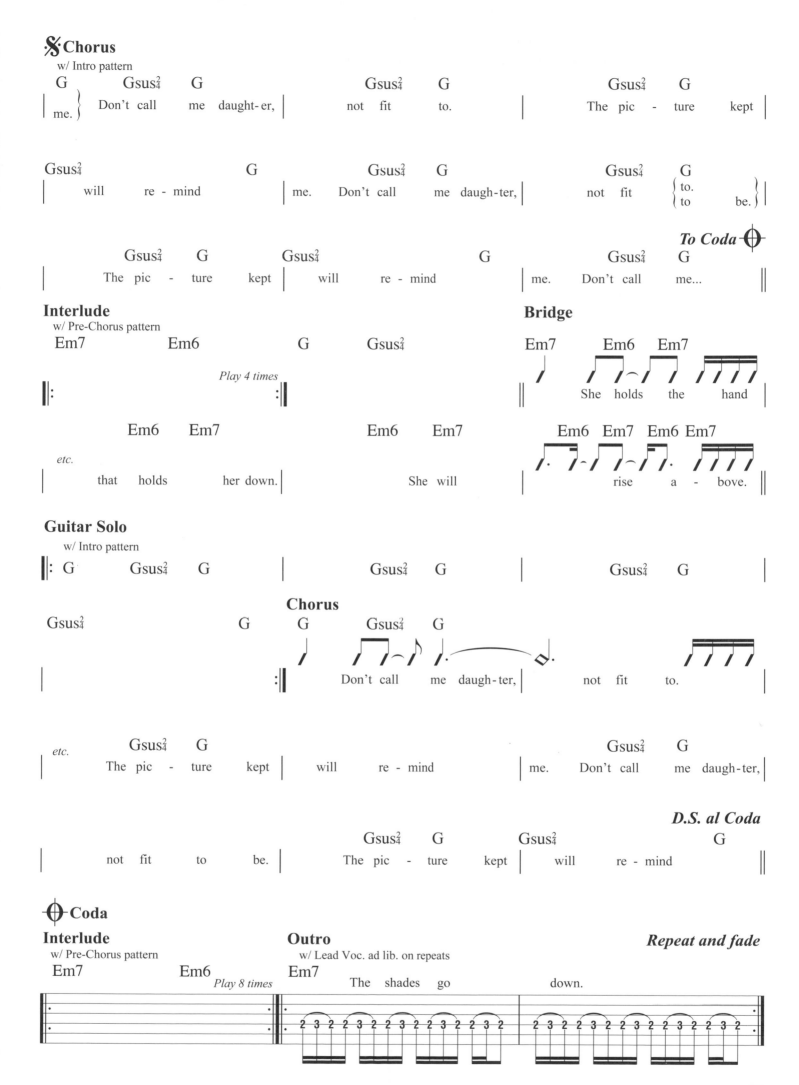

Don't Dream It's Over

Words and Music by Neil Finn

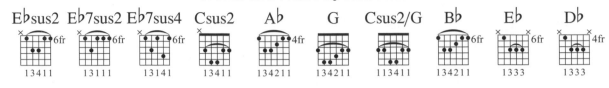

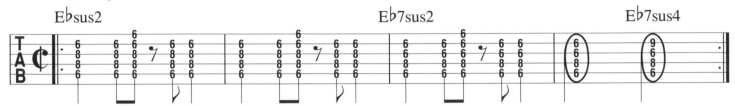

Key of E♭

Intro

Moderately slow, in 2

| E♭sus2 | | | E♭7sus2 | | E♭7sus4 |

𝄋 Verse

E♭sus2   Csus2

etc.

1. There is | free - dom with-in; | there is | free - dom with- out. |
2. Now I'm | tow - ing my car; | there's a | hole in the roof. |
3. *See additional lyrics*

A♭   G   Csus2/G

Try to catch the del |-uge in a pa-per cup. | no proof. |
My pos-ses-sions are caus |-ing me sus-pi-cion but there's | no proof. |

E♭sus2   Csus2

There's a | bat-tle a-head; | man-y | bat-tles are lost, |
In the | pa-per to-day, | tales of | war and of waste, |

A♭   G

but you'll nev-er see the | end of the road while you're | trav - 'ling with me. |
but you turn right o |- ver to the T V page. |

Chorus

*A♭   **B♭   E♭sus2   Csus2

Hey now, hey | now, don't | dream it's | o - ver, hey |

*3rd time, Bass plays F.   **3rd time, Bass plays G.

A♭   B♭   E♭sus2   Csus2

now, hey | now, when the | world comes | in. They |

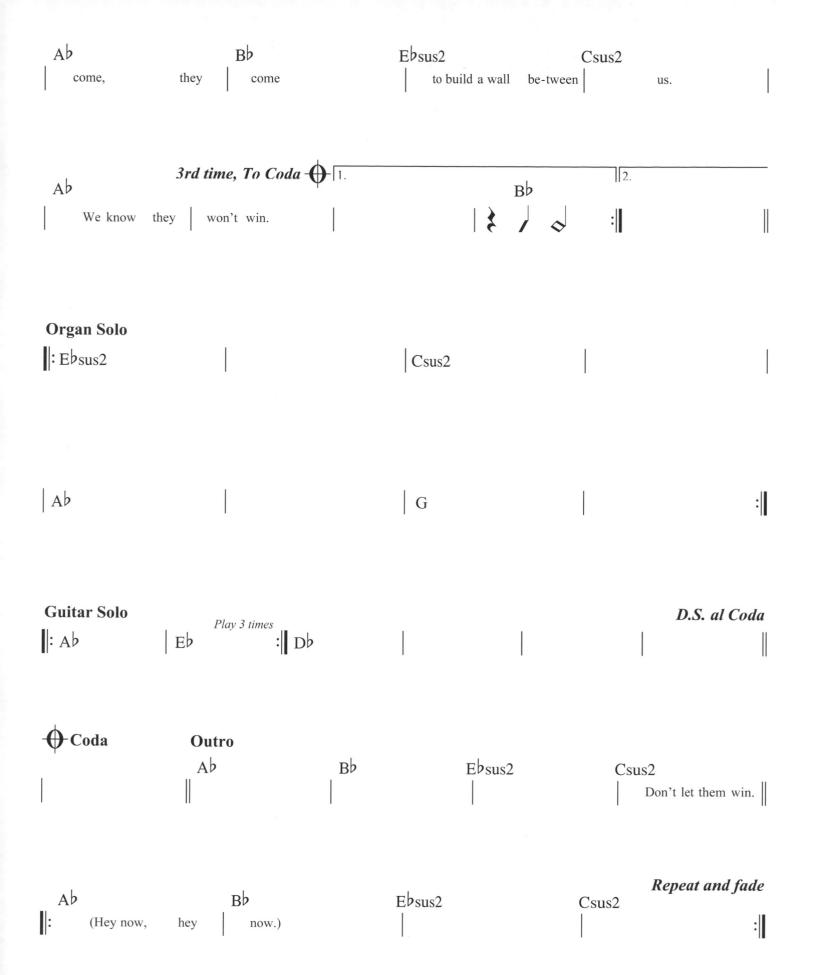

A♭		B♭		E♭sus2		Csus2	
come,	they	come		to build a wall	be-tween	us.	

3rd time, To Coda ⊕ | 1.

A♭						B♭	2.
We know	they	won't win.					

Organic Solo

‖: E♭sus2 | | | Csus2 | | |

| A♭ | | | G | | :‖

Guitar Solo   *D.S. al Coda*

Play 3 times

‖: A♭ | E♭ :‖ D♭ | | | | ‖

⊕ Coda   **Outro**

| A♭ | B♭ | E♭sus2 | Csus2 |
| | | | Don't let them win. ‖

Repeat and fade

| A♭ | B♭ | E♭sus2 | Csus2 |
‖: (Hey now, hey | now.) | | | :‖

Additional Lyrics

3. Now I'm walking again to the beat of a drum,
   And I'm counting the steps to the door of your heart.
   Only shadows ahead barely clearing the roof
   Get to know the feeling of liberation and relief.

Good Riddance (Time of Your Life)

Words by Billie Joe
Music by Green Day

G   Cadd9   D5   Em

Key of G

Intro

Very fast

G   Cadd9   D5

etc.

Verse

1st time, w/ Intro pattern
2nd time, w/ Interlude pattern

G   Cadd9

1. An - oth - er   turn | - ing   point,   a   fork | stuck   in   the |
2. So   take   the   pho | - to - graphs   and   still | - frames   in   your |

D5   G

road. | Time   grabs   you   by | the   wrist,   di - rects |
mind. | Hang   it   on | a   shelf   in   good |

Cadd9   D5   Em

you   where   to | go. | So   make   the   best |
health   and   good | time. | Tat - toos   of   mem - |

D5   Cadd9   G

of   this   test | and   don't   ask   why. |
- o - ries   and   dead | skin   on   tri | - al. |

Em   D5   Cadd9   G

It's   not   a   ques | - tion, but   a   les | - son   learned   in | time. }
For   what   it's   worth, | it   was   worth | all   the | while. }   It's ‖

℠ Chorus

Em   G   Em

some - thing   un - pre - dict | - a - ble,   but | in   the   end   is   right. |

G   Em   D5

| I | hope   you   had   the   time | of   your   life. ‖

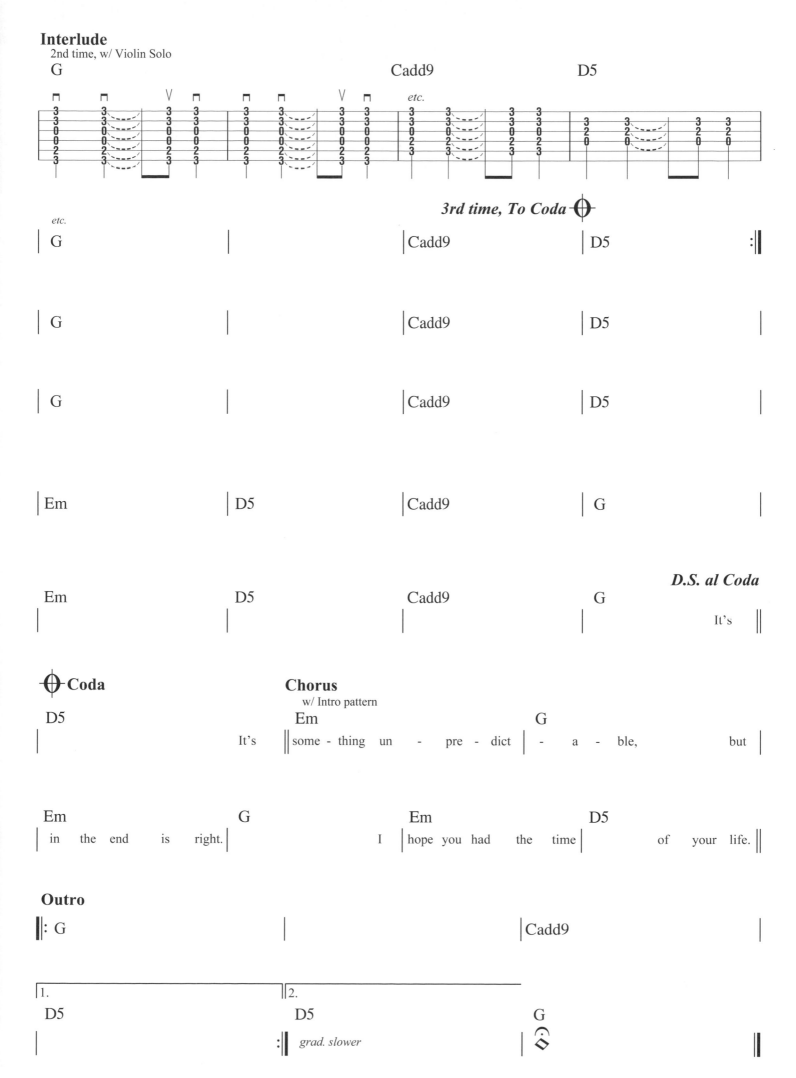

Half of My Heart

Words and Music by John Mayer

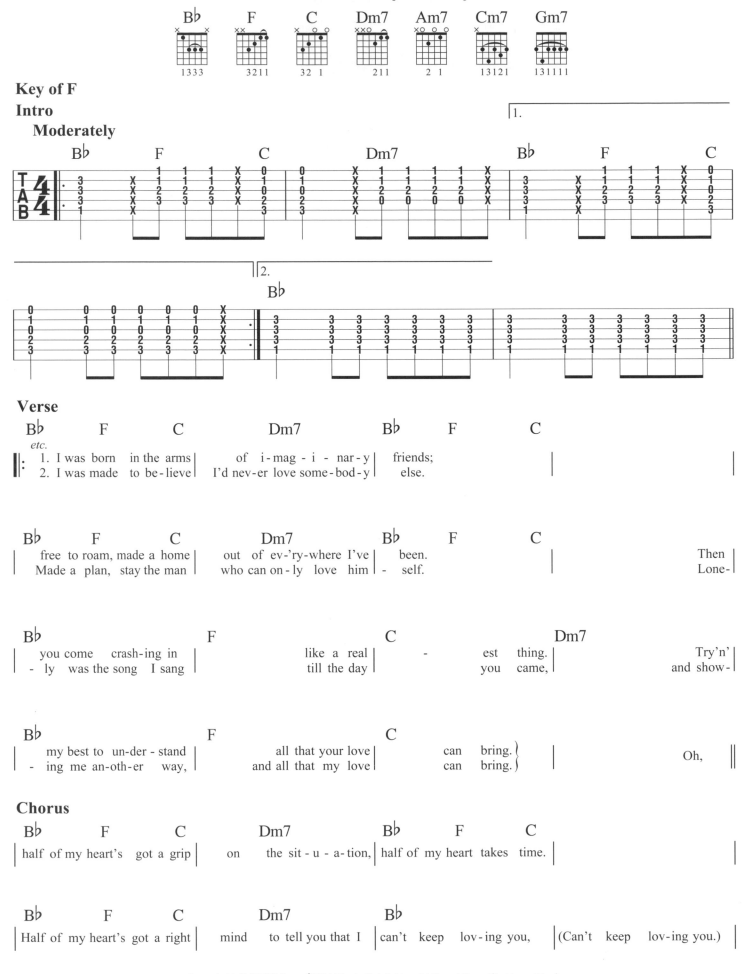

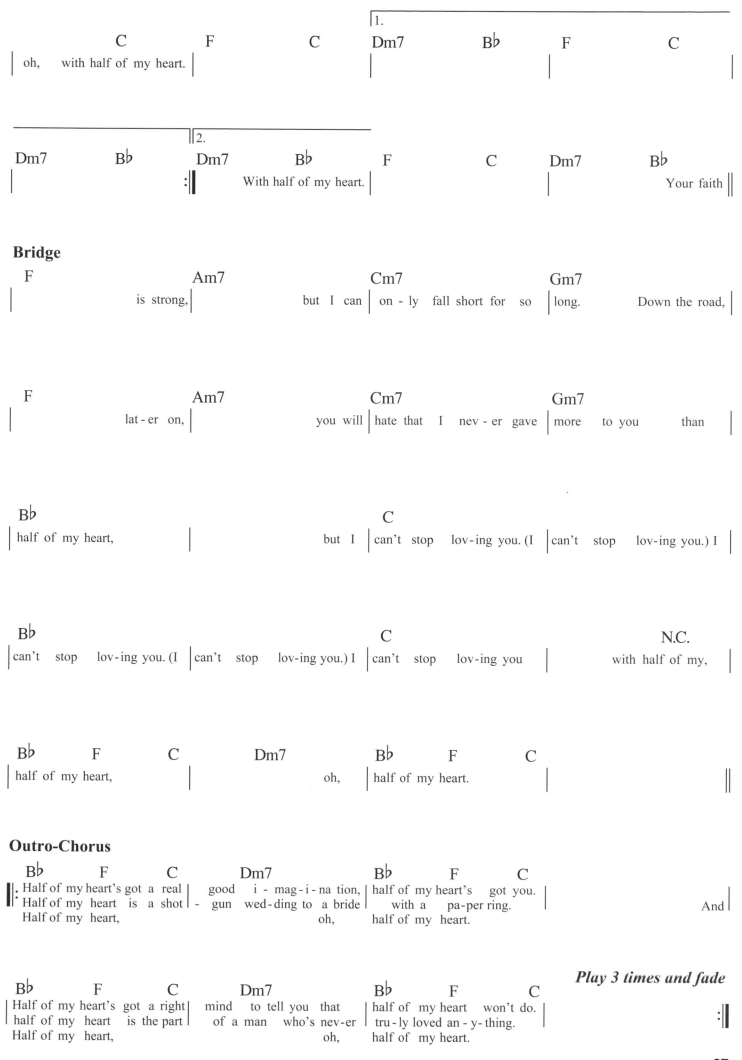

Bridge

Outro-Chorus

Play 3 times and fade

Hey Jude

Words and Music by John Lennon and Paul McCartney

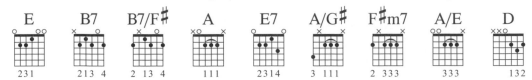

Capo I

Key of F (Capo Key of E)

Verse

Slow

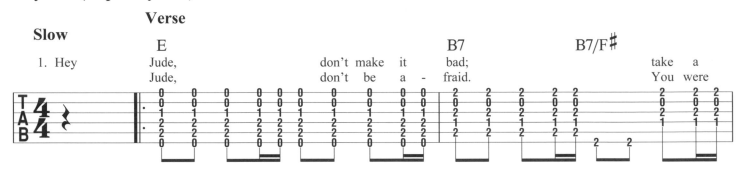

E
1. Hey Jude, don't make it bad; take a
   Jude, don't be a - fraid. You were

B7   B7/F#   E   A
etc.
| sad   song   and make it | bet - ter.   Re - | mem-ber   to let her in - to your
| made   to   go out and | get her.   The | min - ute you let her un - der your

E   B7   B7/F#
| heart;   then you   can   start | to   make   it   bet -
| skin,   then you   be - gin | to   make   it   bet -

1.   2.
E   E   E7
| ter.   2. Hey   : | ter.   And an-y-time you feel the pain,

Bridge

A   A/G#   F#m7   A/E
|| : hey Jude,   re - frain; | don't car   -   ry the world
     hey Jude,   be - gin; | you're wait - ing for some -

B7   E
| -   up - on   your shoul | - ders.
| -   one to   per - form | with.

E7   A   A/G#
| For well   you know   that it's   a fool | who plays   it   cool
| And don't you know   that it's just you? | Hey Jude,   you'll do.

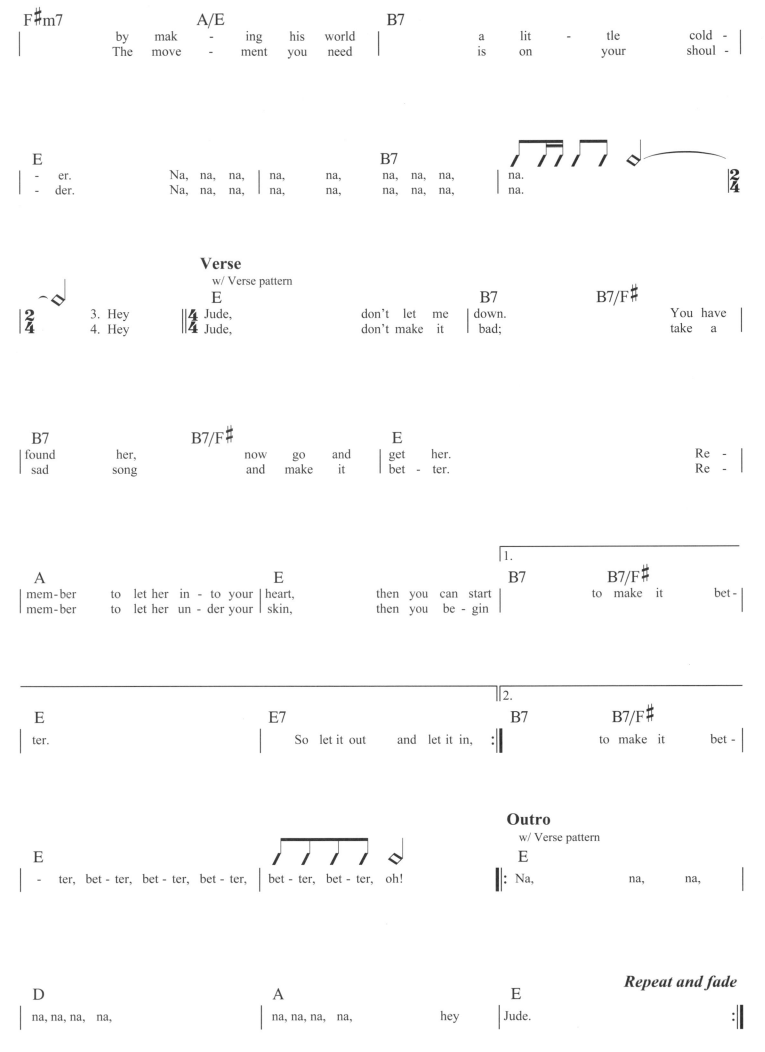

Hey, Soul Sister

Words and Music by Pat Monahan, Espen Lind and Amund Bjorklund

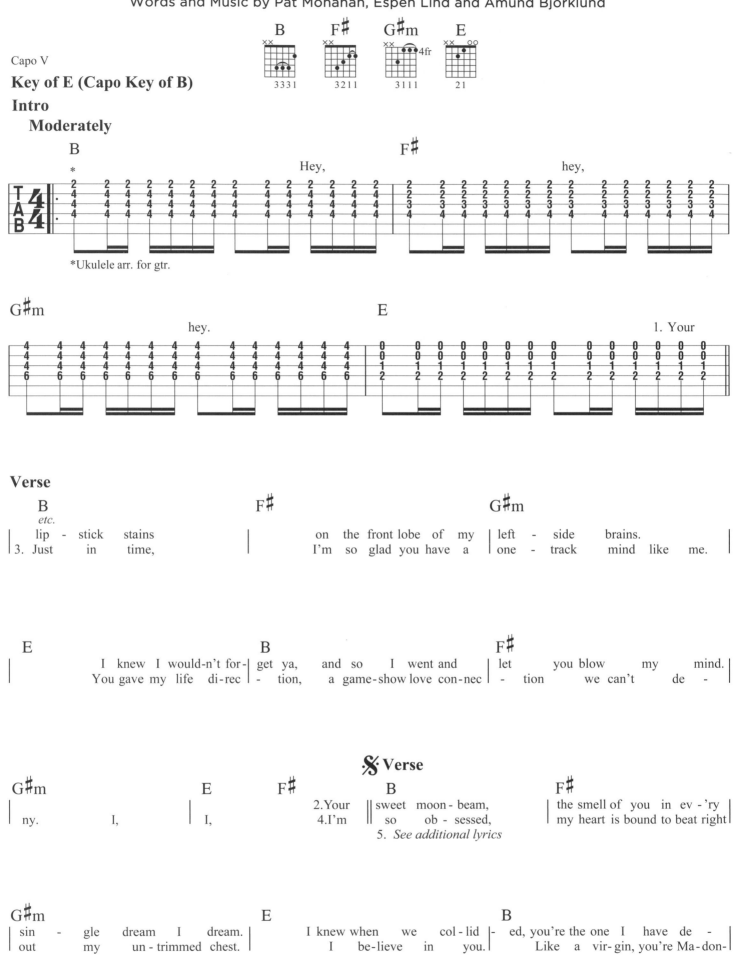

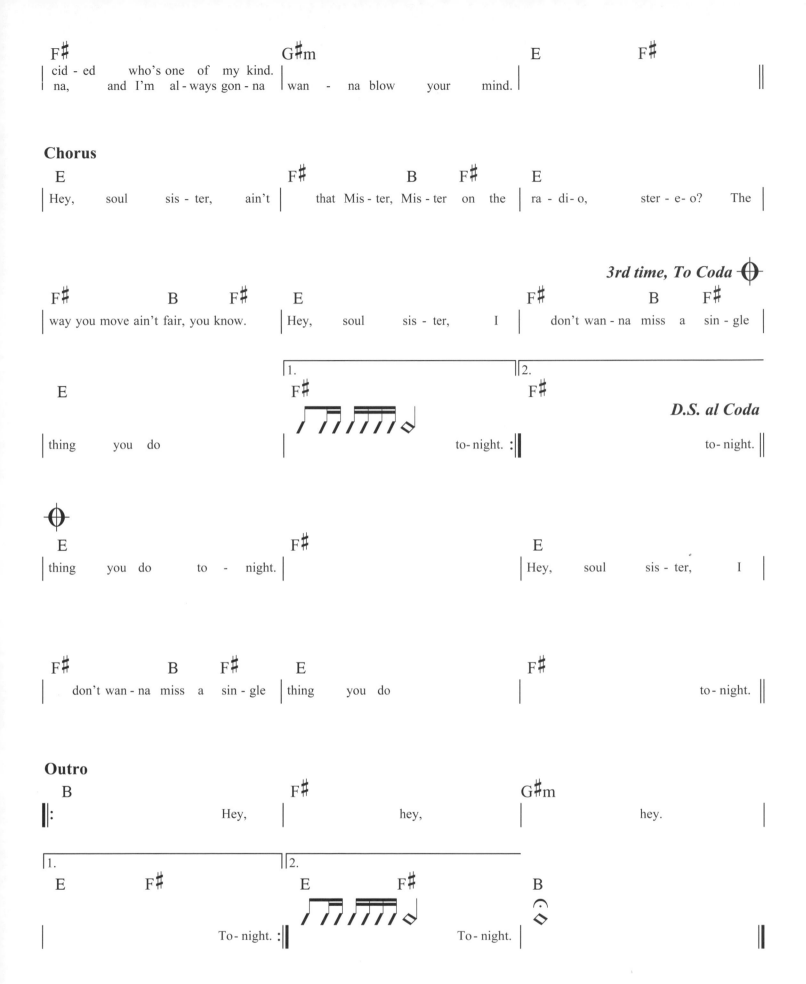

F♯   **G♯m**   **E**   **F♯**

| cid - ed   who's one   of   my   kind. |
| na,   and I'm al - ways gon - na | wan - na blow   your   mind. | ‖

Chorus

E   **F♯**   **B**   **F♯**   **E**

| Hey,   soul   sis - ter,   ain't | that Mis - ter, Mis - ter   on   the | ra - di - o,   ster - e- o?   The |

3rd time, To Coda ⊕

F♯   **B**   **F♯**   **E**   **F♯**   **B**   **F♯**

| way you move ain't fair, you know. | Hey,   soul   sis - ter,   I | don't wan - na miss   a   sin - gle |

E   **1.**   **F♯**   **2.**   **F♯**

D.S. al Coda

| thing   you   do | to- night. :‖ | to- night. ‖

⊕

E   **F♯**   **E**

| thing   you   do   to - night. | Hey,   soul   sis - ter,   I |

F♯   **B**   **F♯**   **E**   **F♯**

| don't wan - na miss   a   sin - gle | thing   you   do | to- night. ‖

Outro

B   **F♯**   **G♯m**

‖:   Hey, | hey, | hey. |

1.   **E**   **F♯**   **2.**   **E**   **F♯**   **B**

| To - night. :‖ | To - night. ‖

Additional Lyrics

5. The way you can cut a rug, watching you's the only drug I need.
    Some gangsta, I'm so thug. You're the only one I'm dreamin' of.
    You see, I can be myself now, finally. In fact, there's nothin' I can't be.
    I want the world to see you'll be with me.

High and Dry

Words and Music by Thomas Yorke, Jonathan Greenwood,
Colin Greenwood, Edward O'Brien and Philip Selway

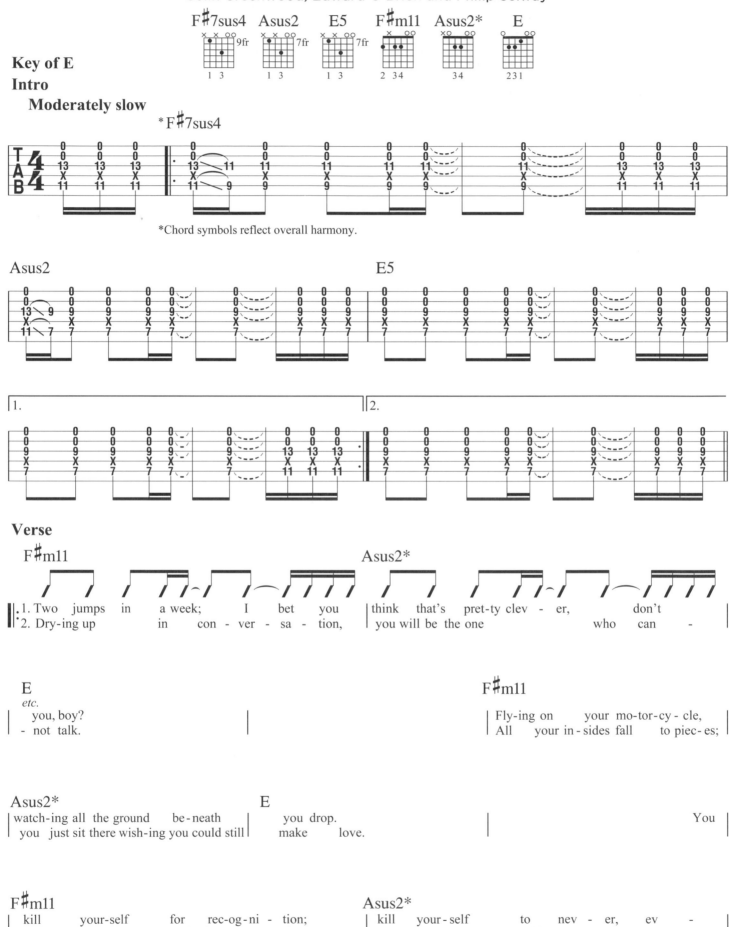

Key of E
Intro
Moderately slow

*Chord symbols reflect overall harmony.

Verse

1. Two jumps in a week; I bet you think that's pret-ty clev - er, don't
2. Dry-ing up in con - ver - sa - tion, you will be the one who can -

you, boy?   Fly-ing on   your mo-tor-cy - cle,
- not talk.   All   your in - sides fall   to piec - es;

watch-ing all the ground be-neath   you drop.   You
you just sit there wish-ing you could still   make   love.

kill   your-self   for rec-og-ni - tion;   kill   your-self   to nev - er, ev -
They're the ones   who'll hate you when you   think   you got the world   all

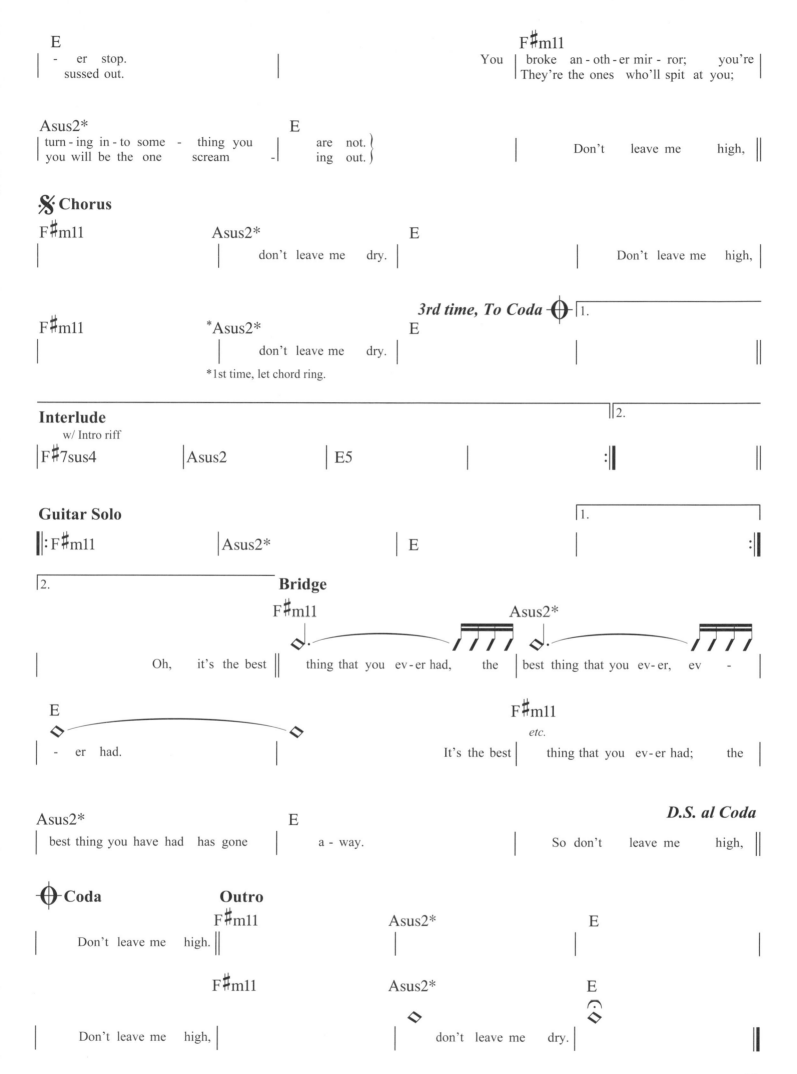

E   F#m11

| - er stop. | You | broke an-oth-er mir-ror; you're |
| sussed out. | | They're the ones who'll spit at you; |

Asus2*   E

| turn-ing in-to some - thing you | are not. | | Don't leave me high, ‖
| you will be the one scream -| ing out. |

𝄋 Chorus

F#m11   Asus2*   E

| | don't leave me dry. | | Don't leave me high, |

F#m11   *Asus2*   ***3rd time, To Coda*** ⊕ |1.

| | don't leave me dry. E | | ‖

*1st time, let chord ring.

Interlude
 w/ Intro riff ||2.

| F#7sus4 | Asus2 | E5 | | :‖ ‖

Guitar Solo   1.

‖: F#m11 | Asus2* | E | | :‖

|2.   **Bridge**

         F#m11   Asus2*

| Oh, it's the best ‖ thing that you ev-er had, the | best thing that you ev-er, ev -

E   F#m11
                 etc.

| - er had. | It's the best | thing that you ev-er had; the |

Asus2*   E   ***D.S. al Coda***

| best thing you have had has gone | a - way. | So don't leave me high, ‖

⊕ **Coda**   **Outro**
       F#m11   Asus2*   E

| Don't leave me high. ‖ | | |

       F#m11   Asus2*   E

| Don't leave me high, | | don't leave me dry. | ‖

Home

Words and Music by Greg Holden and Drew Pearson

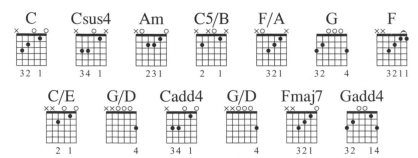

Key of C
Intro
Moderately

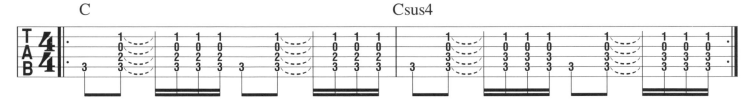

Verse

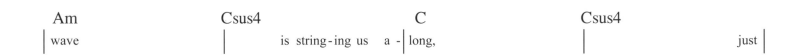

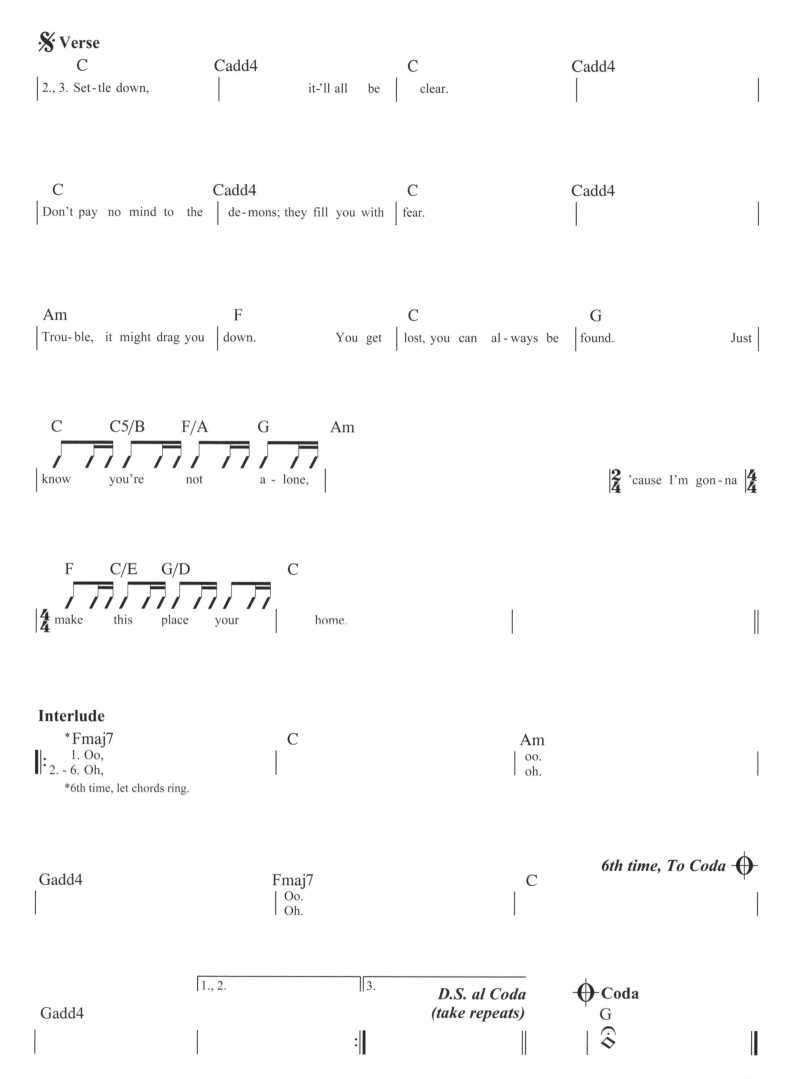

How to Save a Life

Words and Music by Joseph King and Isaac Slade

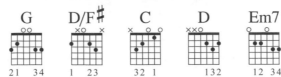

Capo III

Key of B♭ (Capo Key of G)

Intro

Moderately

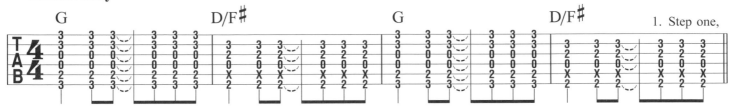

1. Step one,

Verse

G			D/F#			*(Em7)		G	
etc.	you say	we need		to talk.	He	walks, you say,	"Sit
2. Let him	know	that you	know best	'cause	af - ter	all	you
3. *See additional lyrics*						*2nd & 3rd times, substitute chords in parentheses.*

D/F#				G			D/F#		
down, it's just	a talk."		He smiles po - lite	- ly	back at you.
do know best.			Try to slip past	his	de - fense

(Em7) G			D/F#			G		
You stare po - lite	- ly	right on through	some sort of win -
with - out grant - ing	in - no - cence.		Lay down	a

D/F#			(Em7) G			D/F#		
- dow to your right,	as he goes	left and you	stay
list of what is	wrong: the things you've told	him all	a - long.

G			D/F#			(Em7) G		
right be - tween the lines	of fear and blame.	You be - gin to won -
Pray to God he hears	you, and	pray to God he hears

𝄋 Chorus

D/F#			C			D		
- der why you came. And	Where⎫ where⎭ did I go	wrong? I lost a friend
you.							

Em7			G	D/F#	C
some-where a - long	in the bit - ter - ness. And	I would have stayed

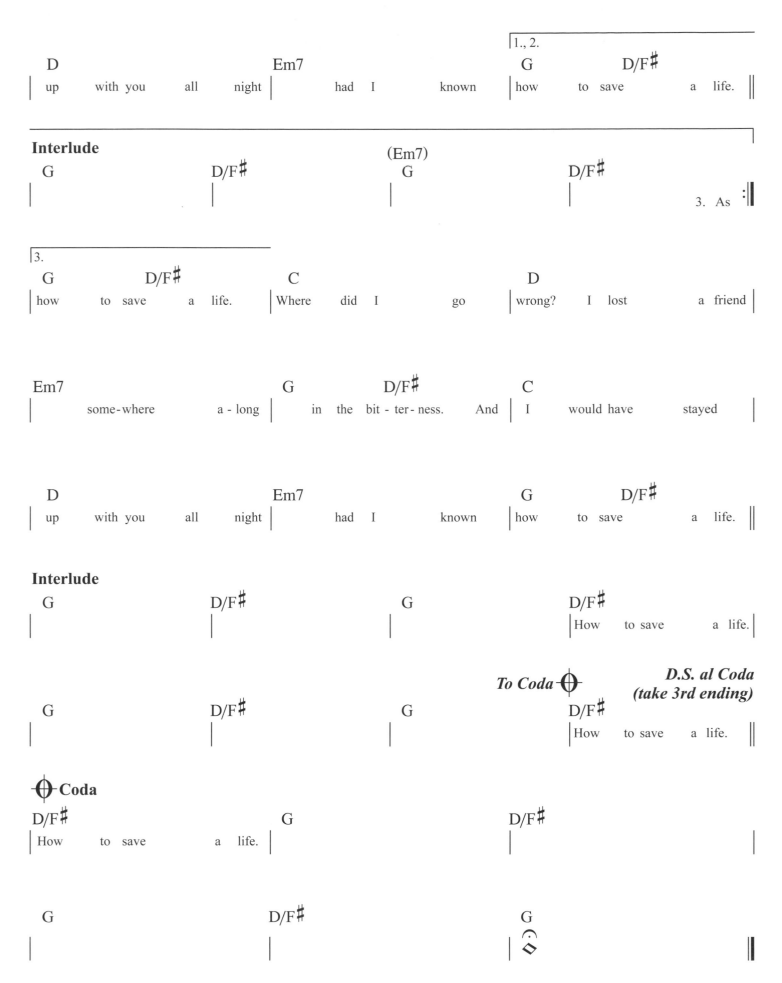

Additional Lyrics

3. As he begins to raise his voice, you lower yours and grant him one last choice:
   Drive until you lose the road or break with the ones you've followed.
   He will do one of two things: he will admit to ev'rything
   Or he'll say he's just not the same and you'll begin to wonder why you came.

I Can See Clearly Now

Words and Music by Johnny Nash

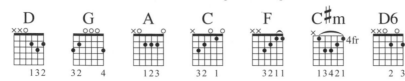

Key of D

Verse

Moderately

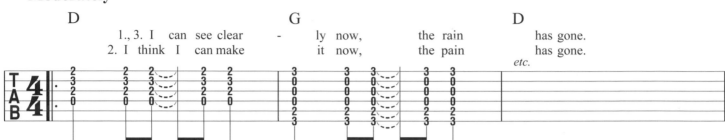

> 1., 3. I can see clear - ly now, the rain has gone.
> 2. I think I can make it now, the pain has gone.

etc.

> I can see all   ob - sta - cles
> All of the bad   feel - ings have

> in my   way.   Gone are the dark
> dis - ap - peared.   Here is that rain -

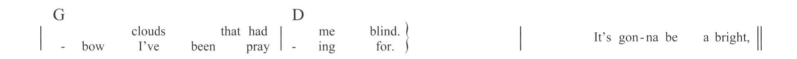

> - bow   clouds   that had   me   blind. }   It's gon-na be   a bright,
> - bow   I've been pray   - ing   for. }

Chorus

Half-time feel   **End half-time feel**   *3rd time, To Coda* ⊕

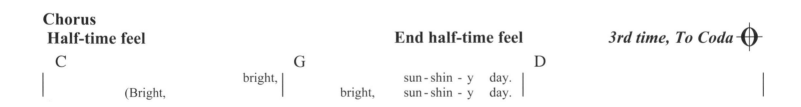

> bright,   sun - shin - y   day.
> (Bright,   bright,   sun - shin - y   day.

1.

Half-time feel   **End half-time feel**

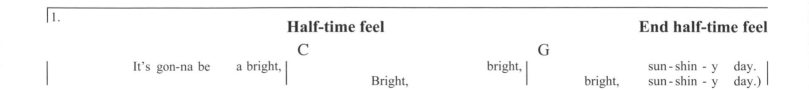

> It's gon-na be   a bright,   bright,   sun - shin - y   day.
> Bright,   bright,   sun - shin - y   day.)

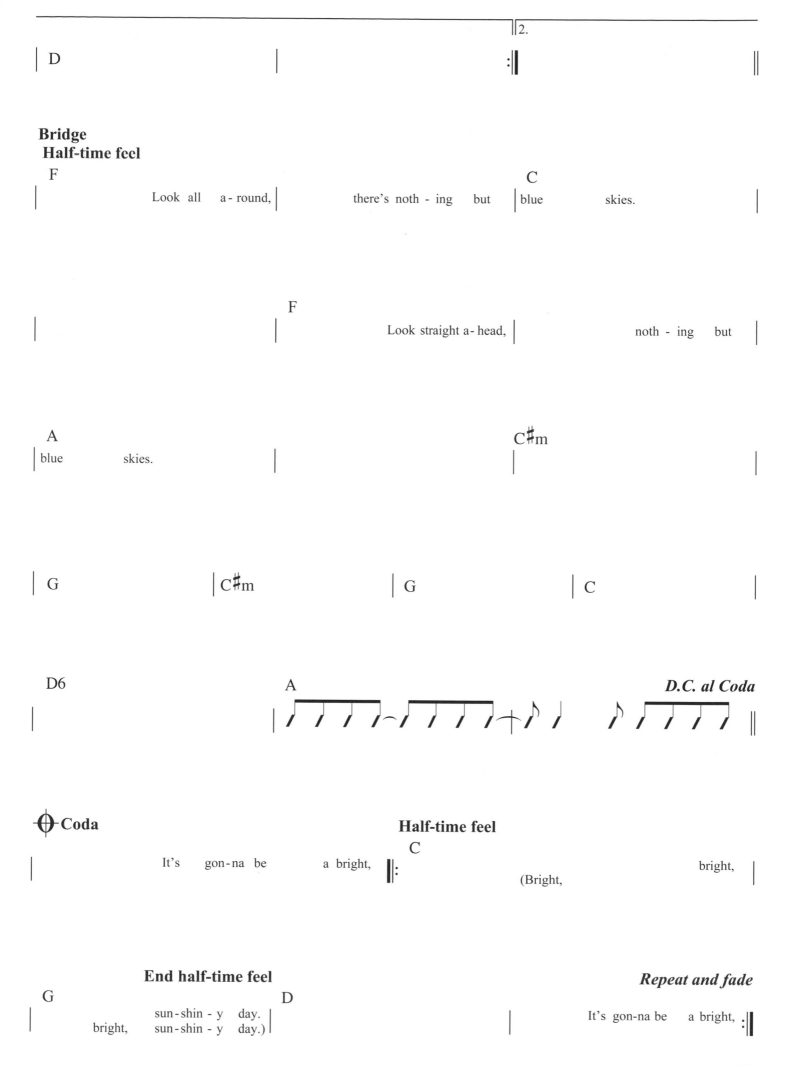

39

I Will Follow You Into the Dark

Words and Music by Benjamin Gibbard

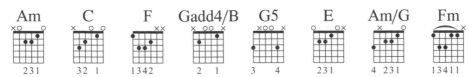

Capo V

Key of F (Capo Key of C)

Intro

Fast

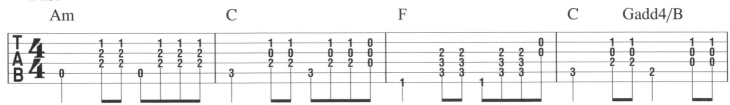

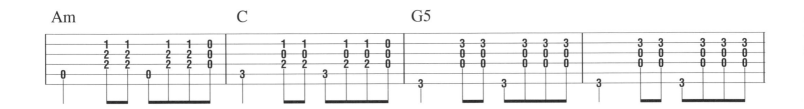

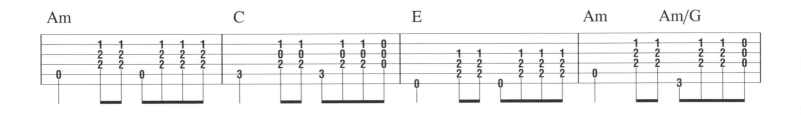

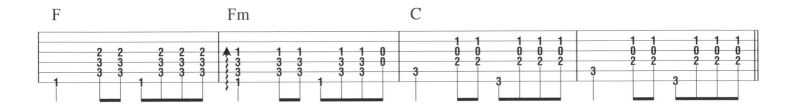

𝄋 Verse

w/ Intro picking style

C			Am		
1. Love	of	mine,	some - day	you will	die,	but I'll be
Cath - 'lic	school,		as vi - cious as	Rom - an	rule,	I got my
3. You	and	me,	have seen ev - 'ry - thing	to	see	from Ban - kok to

F			C		G5
close	be - hind.		I'll fol - low	you	in - to the dark.	No
knuck - les	bruised		by a la	- dy in black.	And I
Cal - ga - ry,		and the soles	of your shoes	are

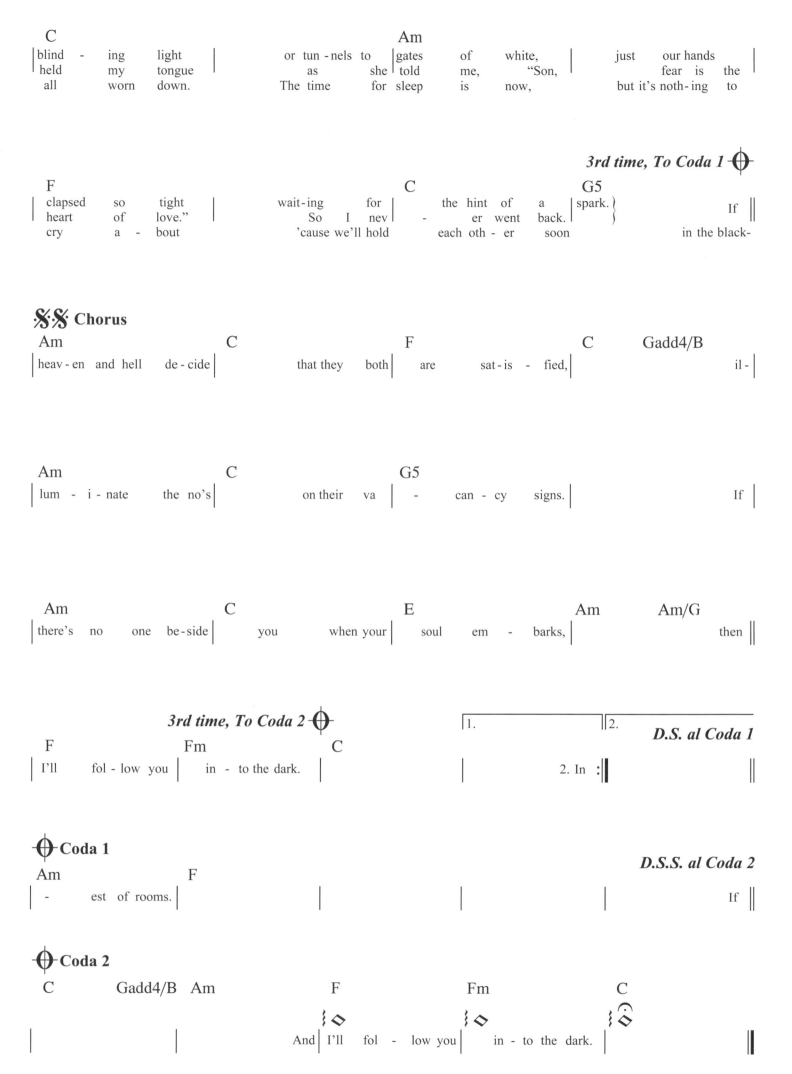

I Will Wait

Words and Music by Mumford & Sons

Open D tuning, down 1/2 step:
(low to high) D♭-A♭-D♭-F-A♭-D♭

Key of D
Intro

Moderately fast

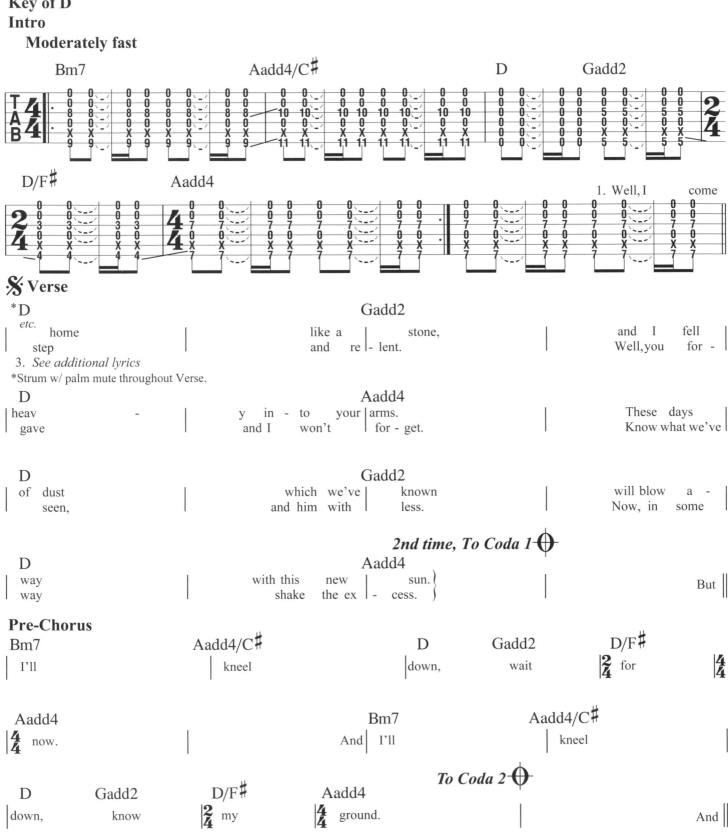

*Strum w/ palm mute throughout Verse.

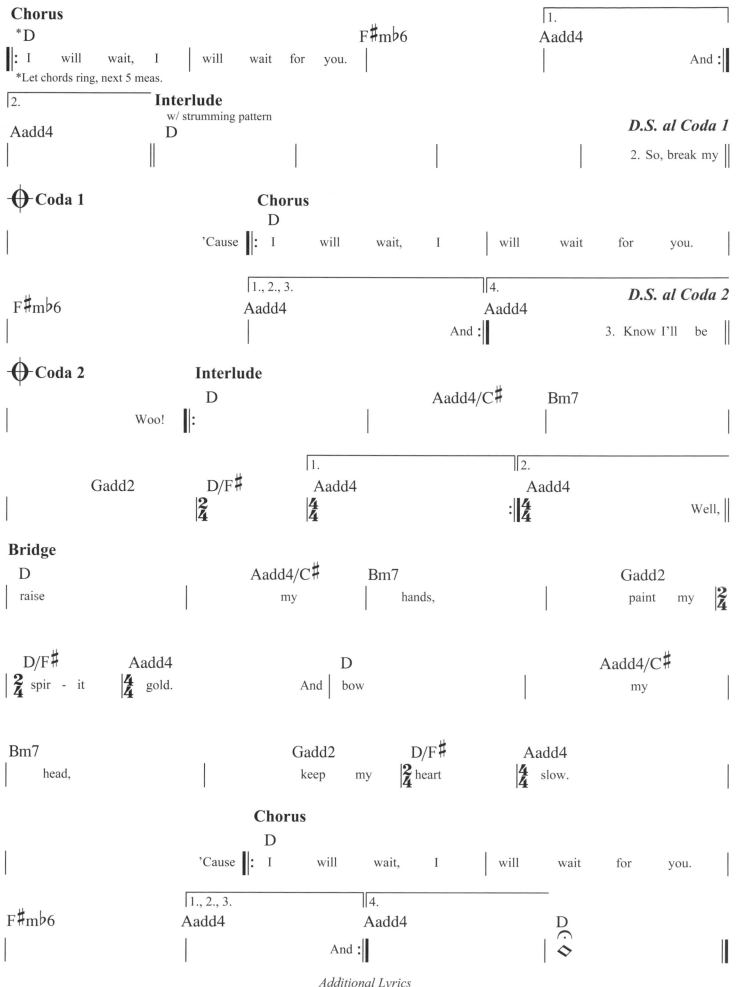

Chorus

D   F#m♭6   **1.** Aadd4

‖: I will wait, I | will wait for you. | | And :‖

*Let chords ring, next 5 meas.

2. Aadd4   **Interlude**

w/ strumming pattern   ***D.S. al Coda 1***

D

| ‖ | | | 2. So, break my ‖

⊕ Coda 1   **Chorus**

D

'Cause ‖: I will wait, I | will wait for you. |

F#m♭6   **1., 2., 3.** Aadd4   **4.** Aadd4   ***D.S. al Coda 2***

| | And :‖ 3. Know I'll be ‖

⊕ Coda 2   **Interlude**

D   Aadd4/C#   Bm7

| Woo! ‖: | | |

Gadd2   D/F#   **1.** Aadd4   **2.** Aadd4

| $\frac{2}{4}$ $\frac{4}{4}$ | :‖ $\frac{4}{4}$ | Well, ‖

Bridge

D   Aadd4/C#   Bm7   Gadd2

| raise | my | hands, | paint my $\frac{2}{4}$

D/F#   Aadd4   D   Aadd4/C#

$\frac{2}{4}$ spir - it $\frac{4}{4}$ gold. | And | bow | my |

Bm7   Gadd2   D/F#   Aadd4

| head, | | keep my $\frac{2}{4}$ heart $\frac{4}{4}$ slow. |

Chorus

D

'Cause ‖: I will wait, I | will wait for you. |

F#m♭6   **1., 2., 3.** Aadd4   **4.** Aadd4   D

| | And :‖ | ◇ | ‖

Additional Lyrics

3. Know I'll be bold as well as strong,
    And use my head alongside my heart.
    So take my flesh and fix my eyes,
    A tethered mind free from the lies.

I'm Yours

Words and Music by Jason Mraz

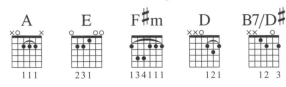

Capo II

Key of B (Capo Key of A)

Intro

Moderately slow

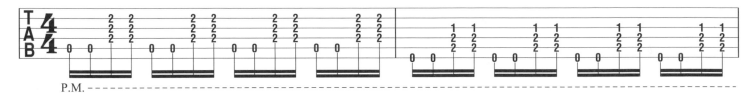

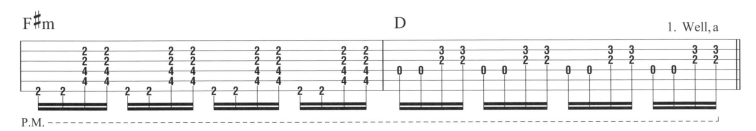

1. Well, a

%Verse

A   *etc.*

| you done done me in; you bet I felt it. I | tried to be chill,   but you're so hot that I melt - ed. I |
| way too long check-ing my tongue in   the mir-ror and | bend-ing o-ver back-wards just to try to see it clear-er But |

F#m   D

| fell right through the cracks.   Now I'm | try-ing to get back.   Be - fore the |
| my breath fogged up the glass,   and so I | drew a new face and I laughed.   I |

A   E

| cool done run out, I'll be giv-ing it my best-est and | noth-ing's gon-na stop me but di-vine in-ter-ven-tion.   I |
| guess what I'll be say-ing is there ain't no bet-ter rea-son to | rid your-self of van-i-ties and just go with the sea-sons. It's |

F#m   D

| reck on it's a-gain my turn   to | win some or learn some. } But |
| what we aim to do. Our | name is our vir - tue. } |

Chorus

A   E   F#m   D

| I won't hes - i - | tate no more, no | more. It can - not | wait. I'm yours. |

1st time only

Interlude

| A | E | F#m | D |

Verse

A   E

| 2. Well, open up your mind and see like | me. Open up your plans and, damn, you're |
| 4. Well, open up your mind and see like | me. Open up your plans and, damn, you're |

F#m   D

| free. A, look into your heart and you'll find | love, love, love, love. |
| free. A, look into your heart and you'll find that | the sky is yours. So |

A   E

| Lis-ten to the mu-sic of the mo-ment; peo-ple dance and | sing. We're just one big fam-i- |
| please don't, please don't, please don't... There's no | need to com - pli - cate 'cause our |

To Coda ✪

F#m   D

| ly, and it's our god - for-sak-en right to be | loved, loved, loved, loved, |
| time is short. This, oo, this, oo, this is our | fate. I'm loved yours. |

Chorus

N.C.(B7/D#)   A   E   F#m

| loved. So ‖ I won't hes - i - | tate no more, no | more. It can - not |

D   A   E   F#m

| wait. I'm sure there's no | need to com - pli - | cate. Our time is | short. This is our |

Interlude

D   A   E   F#m   E

| fate. I'm yours. *Scat...* ‖: | *(1st time only:)* Skooch on o - ver |

                 1.   2.   *D.S. al Coda*

D   B7/D#   N.C. B7/D#   N.C.

| clos - er, dear, and I will nib-ble your | ear. :‖ | 3. I've been spend-ing ‖ |

✪ **Coda**

Outro   *Repeat and fade*

*B7/D# N.C.   A   E   F#m   D

| *Scat...* ‖: | | | :‖ |

*Let chord ring.

Iris

from the Motion Picture CITY OF ANGELS
Words and Music by John Rzeznik

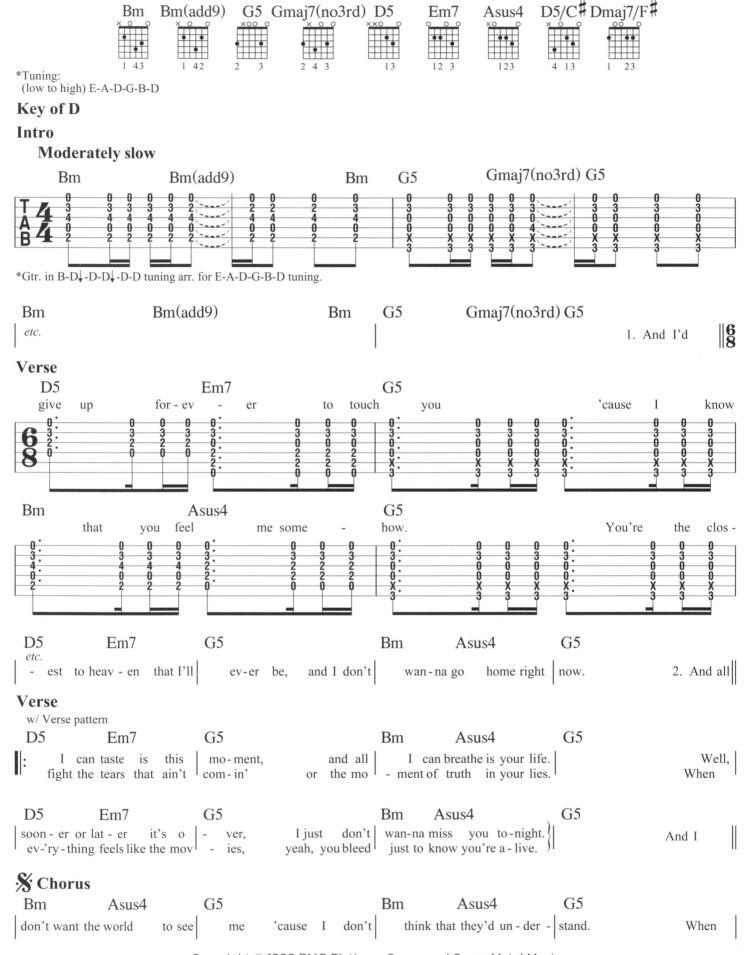

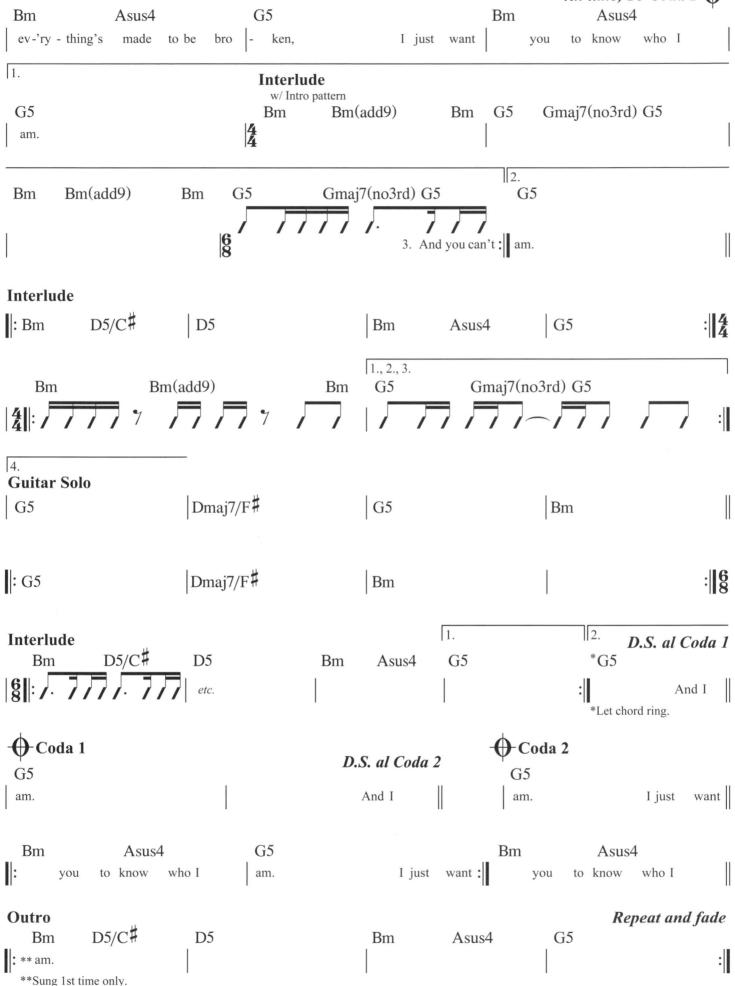

Island in the Sun

Words and Music by Rivers Cuomo

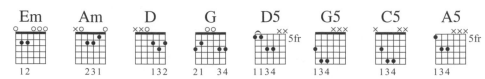

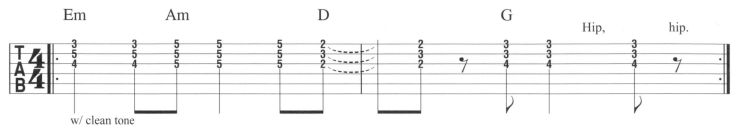

Key of G

Intro

Moderately

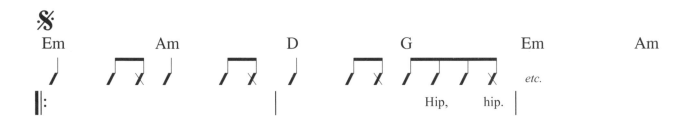

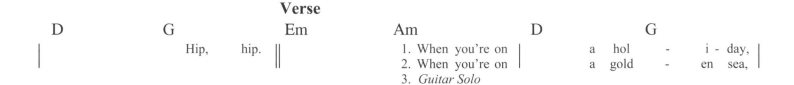

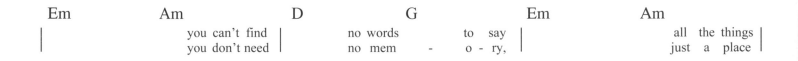

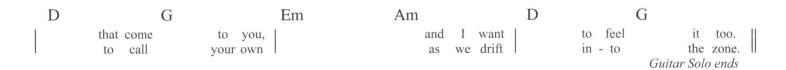

Chorus

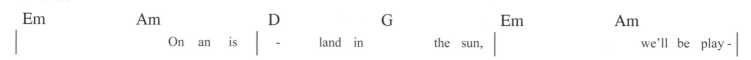

Em   Am   D   G   Em   Am

On an is - land in the sun, we'll be play -

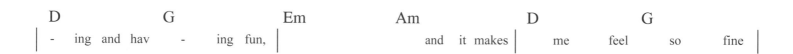

D   G   Em   Am   D   G

- ing and hav - ing fun, and it makes me feel so fine

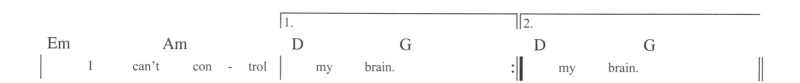

Em   Am   D   G   D   G

1. I can't con - trol my brain. 2. my brain.

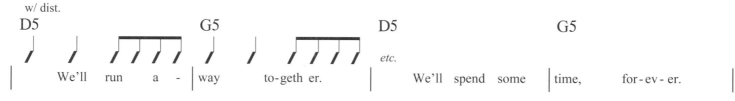

Bridge

w/ dist.

D5   G5   D5   G5

We'll run a - way to-geth er. *etc.* We'll spend some time, for-ev - er.

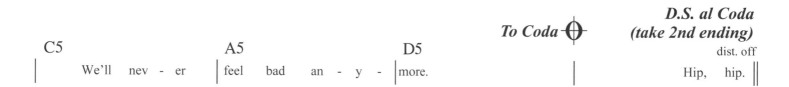

To Coda ⊕   **D.S. al Coda**
(take 2nd ending)
dist. off

C5   A5   D5

We'll nev - er feel bad an - y - more. Hip, hip.

⊕ **Coda**   **Outro**

dist. off   Em   Am   D   G

Hip, hip. We'll nev -

Repeat and fade

Em   Am   D   G   Em   Am   D   G

etc.
- er feel bad an - y - more. No, no.

Learning to Fly

Words and Music by Tom Petty and Jeff Lynne

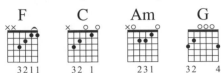

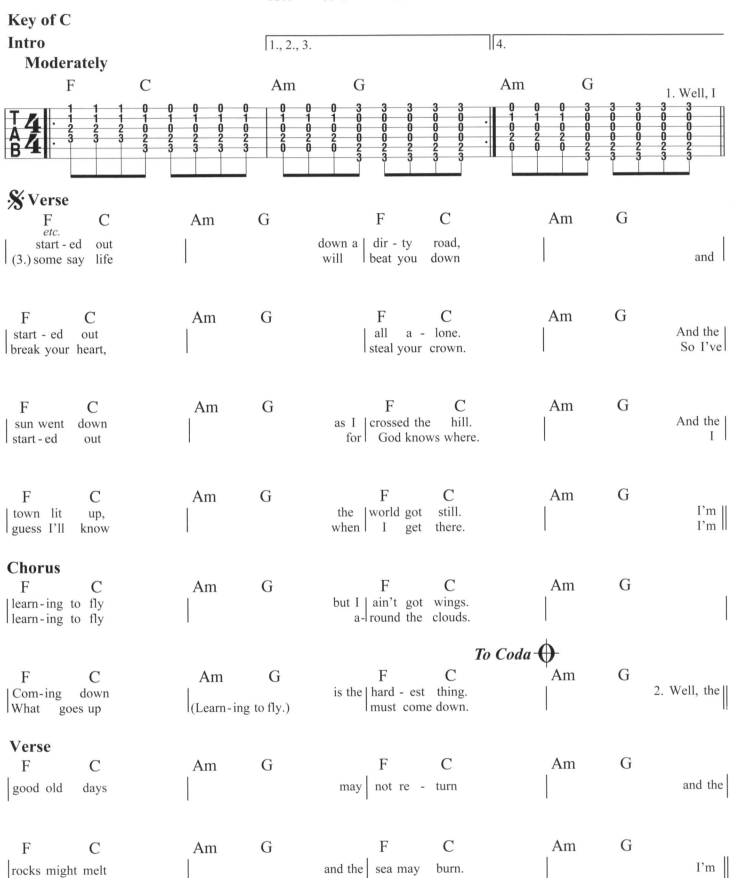

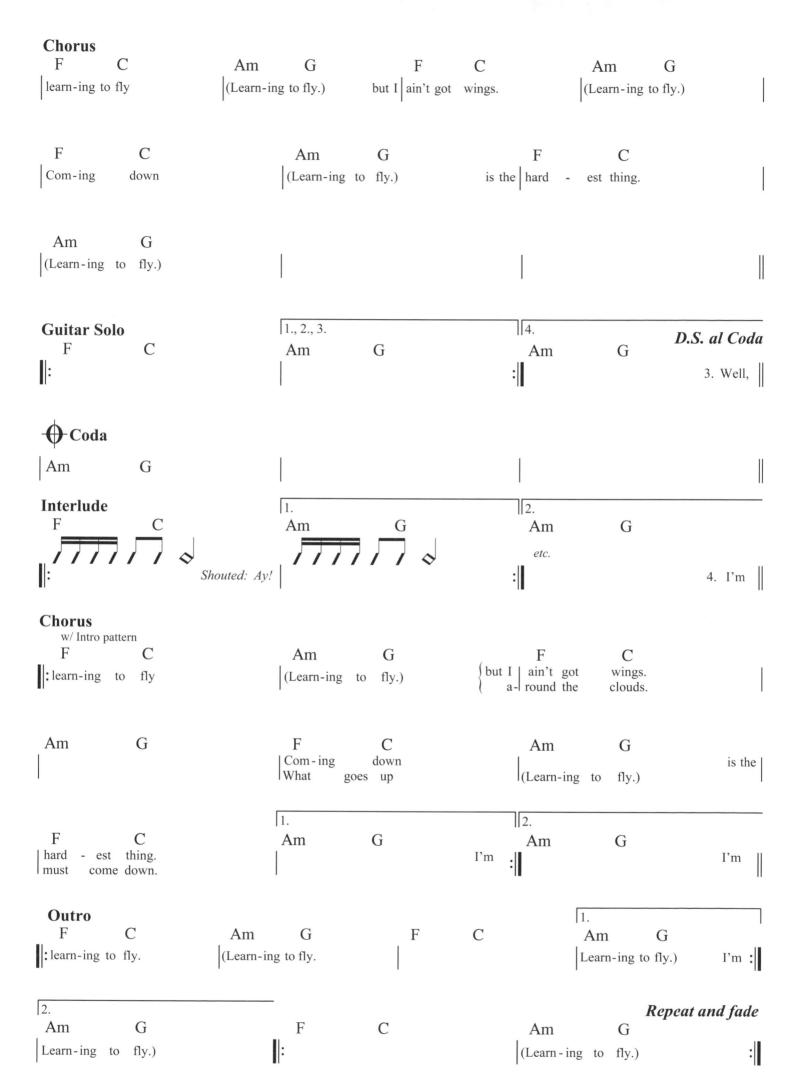

Listen to the Music

Words and Music by Tom Johnston

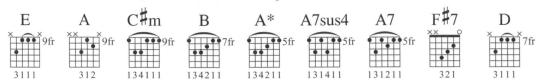

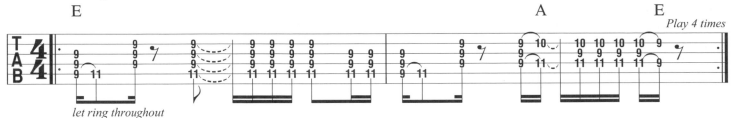

Key of E
Intro
    Moderately

let ring throughout

Verse

	E		A	E
etc.				
1. Don't you feel it grow - in'	day by day?		Peo-ple	get-tin' read y for the
3. Well, I know you know bet-ter,	ev-'ry-thing I say.		Meet me in the coun-try for	a day.

C#m		B		A*	
news.	Some are	hap - py;	some are	sad.	Whoa,
	We'll be	hap - py,	and we'll	dance,	Lord,

A7sus4	A7	E		A	E
we're gon-na let the mu-sic	play.		Mm.		
we're gon-na dance the blues a-way.					4. But,

Verse

E		A	E
2. What the peo - ple need is a	way to make 'em smile.		It
if I'm feel-in' good to you and you're	feel-in' good to me,		

	C#m	
ain't so hard to do if you know how.		Got - ta get a
there ain't noth - in' we can't do or say.		Feel - in'

B		A*	
mes - sage,	get it on	through.	Lord,
good,	feel - in'	fine.	Whoa,

A7sus4	A7	E	
now, ma - ma, go-in' to af - ter 'while.			Oh,
ba - by, let the mu-sic play.			

Chorus

C#m   A*

whoa,   lis - ten to the   mu - sic.   Oh,

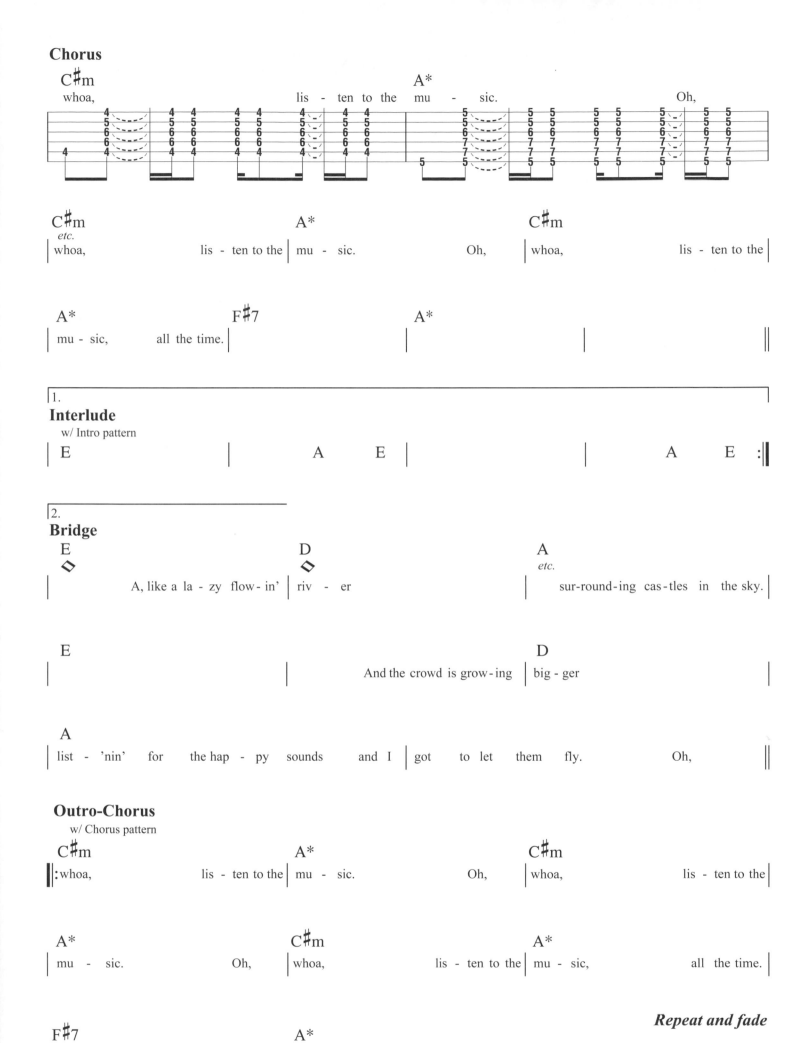

C#m   A*   C#m

etc.

whoa,   lis - ten to the | mu - sic.   Oh, | whoa,   lis - ten to the |

A*   F#7   A*

| mu - sic,   all the time. | | ||

1.

Interlude

w/ Intro pattern

| E | A   E | | A   E :|

2.

Bridge

E   D   A

◇   ◇   *etc.*

| A, like a la - zy flow - in' | riv - er   sur-round-ing cas - tles in the sky. |

E   D

| | And the crowd is grow - ing | big - ger |

A

| list - 'nin'   for   the hap - py   sounds   and I | got   to let   them fly.   Oh, ||

Outro-Chorus

w/ Chorus pattern

C#m   A*   C#m

|: whoa,   lis - ten to the | mu - sic.   Oh, | whoa,   lis - ten to the |

A*   C#m   A*

| mu - sic.   Oh, | whoa,   lis - ten to the | mu - sic,   all the time. |

Repeat and fade

F#7   A*

| | | Oh,   :|

Losing My Religion

Words and Music by William Berry, Peter Buck, Michael Mills and Michael Stipe

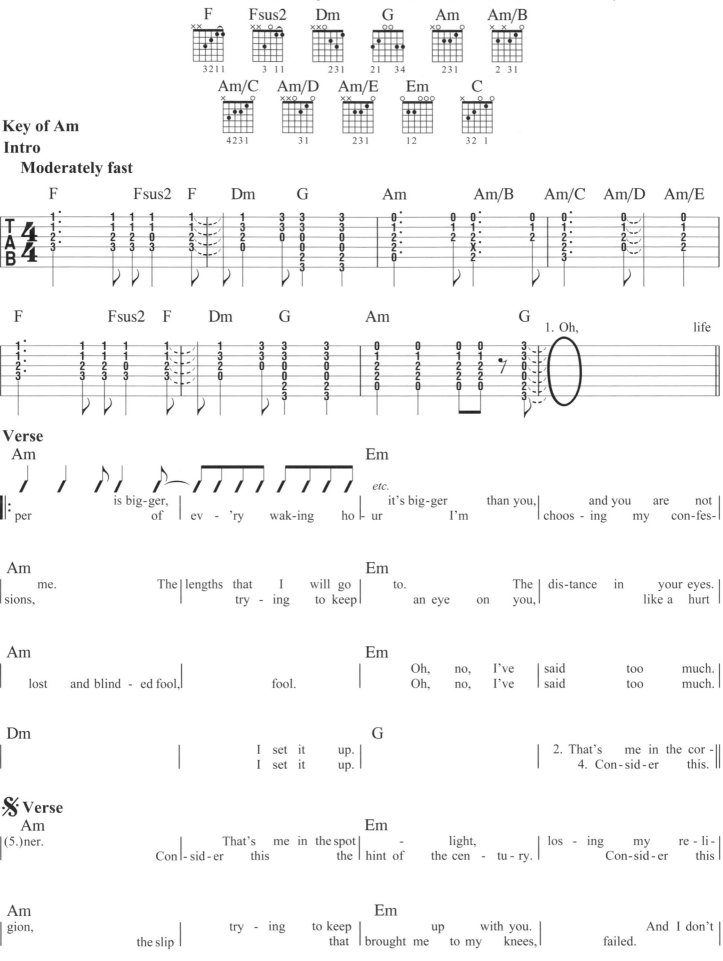

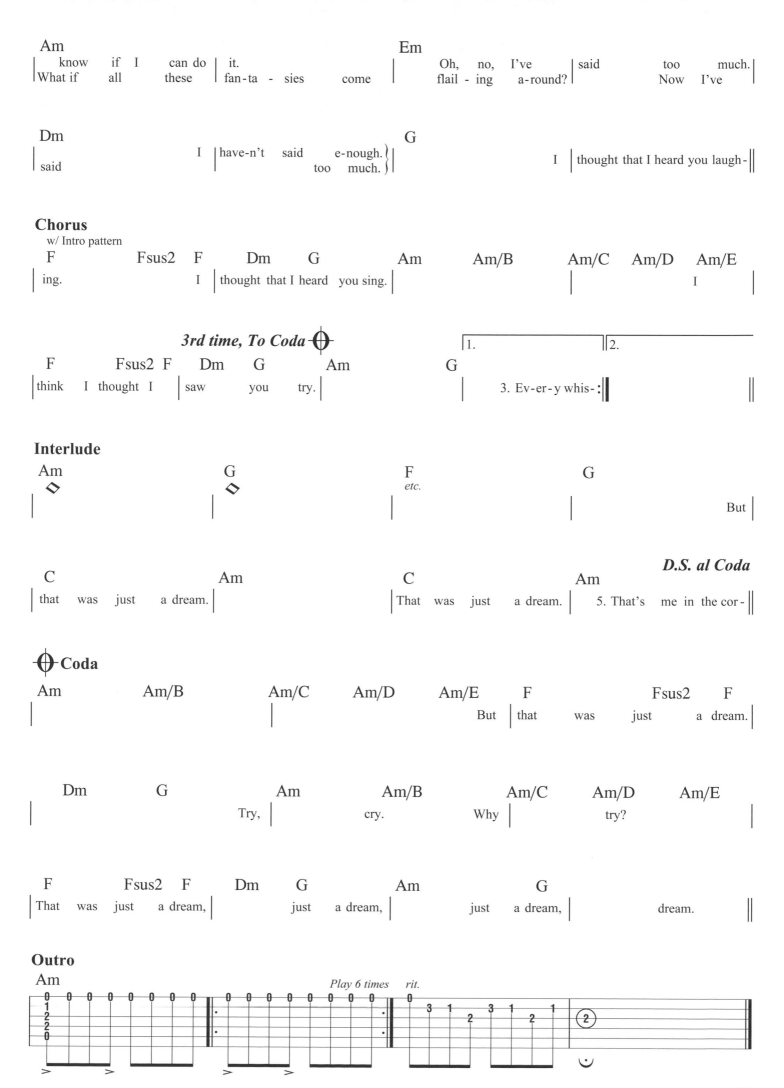

Maggie May

Words and Music by Rod Stewart and Martin Quittenton

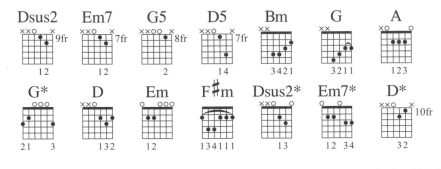

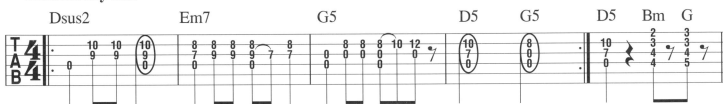

Key of D

Intro

Moderately fast

𝄋 Verse

A	G*	D			
1. Wake up, Mag-gie, I	think I got some-thin' to	say to you.			It's
2., 3., 4. *See additional lyrics*					

A	G*	D		
late Sep - tem-ber and I	real - ly should be back	at school.			I

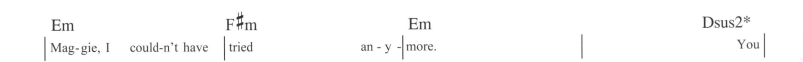

G*	D	G*	A	
know I keep you a-mused,	but I	feel I'm be - ing used.			Oh,

Em	F#m	Em	Dsus2*
Mag-gie, I could-n't have	tried an - y -more.		You

Em	A	Em	A	
led me a-way from	home just to	save ya from be-ing a -	lone.	You

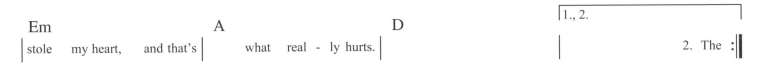

1., 2.

Em	A	D	2. The :
stole my heart, and that's	what real - ly hurts.		

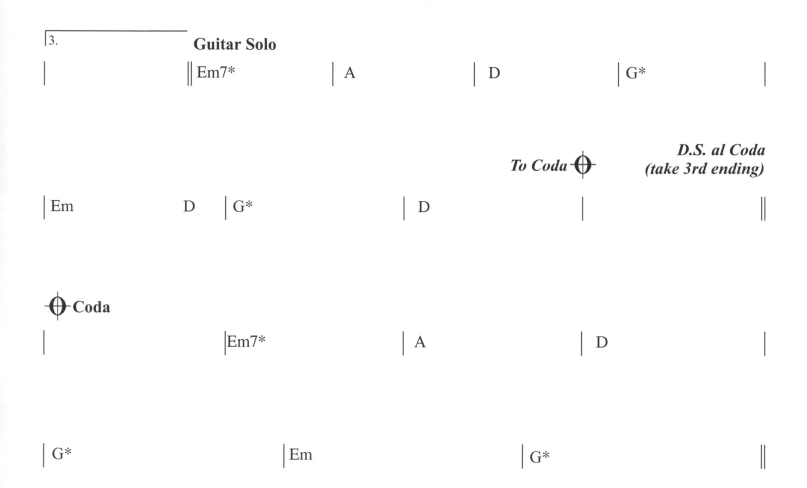

Guitar Solo

| 3. | | Em7* | A | D | G* |

To Coda ⊕

D.S. al Coda
(take 3rd ending)

| Em | D | G* | D | |

⊕ **Coda**

| | Em7* | A | D | |

| G* | Em | G* | |

Outro

Repeat and fade

D*   Em7   G5   D*

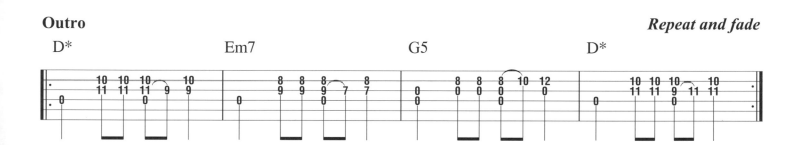

Additional Lyrics

2. The mornin' sun, when it's in your face, really shows your age.
   But that don't worry me none, in my eyes, you're ev'rything.
   I laughed at all of your jokes. My love, you didn't need to coax.
   Oh, Maggie, I couldn't have tried anymore.
   You led me away from home just to save ya from bein' alone.
   You stole my soul, and that's a pain I can do without.

3. All I needed was a friend to lend a guiding hand.
   But you turned into a lover and, mother, what a lover, you wore me out.
   All you did was wreck my bed and, in the mornin', kicked me in the head.
   Oh, Maggie, I couldn't have tried anymore.
   You led me away from home 'cause you didn't want to be alone.
   You stole my heart, I couldn't leave ya if I tried.

4. I suppose I could collect my books and get on back to school
   Or steal my Daddy's cue and make a living out of playin' pool
   Or find myself a rock and roll band that needs a helpin' hand.
   Oh, Maggie, I wished I'd never seen your face.
   You made a first-class fool out of me but I'm as blind as a fool can be.
   You stole me heart but I love ya anyway.

Mrs. Robinson

from THE GRADUATE
Words and Music by Paul Simon

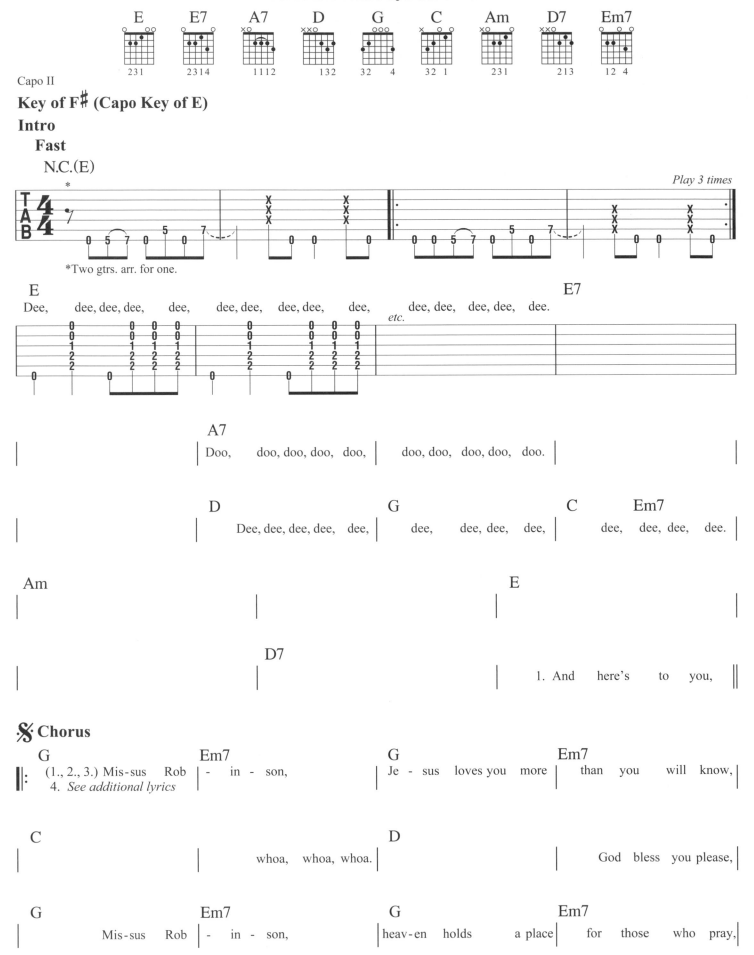

Capo II

Key of F♯ (Capo Key of E)

Intro

Fast

N.C.(E)

Play 3 times

*Two gtrs. arr. for one.

E — Dee, dee, dee, dee, dee, dee, dee, dee, dee, dee, *etc.* dee, dee, dee, dee, dee. E7

A7 — Doo, doo, doo, doo, doo, doo, doo, doo, doo, doo.

D — Dee, dee, dee, dee, dee, G — dee, dee, dee, dee, C — dee, dee, dee, dee. Em7

Am   E

D7   1. And here's to you,

𝄋 Chorus

G (1., 2., 3.) Mis-sus Rob Em7 - in - son,   G Je - sus loves you more Em7 than you will know,
4. *See additional lyrics*

C   whoa, whoa, whoa.   D   God bless you please,

G Mis-sus Rob Em7 - in - son,   G heav-en holds a place Em7 for those who pray,

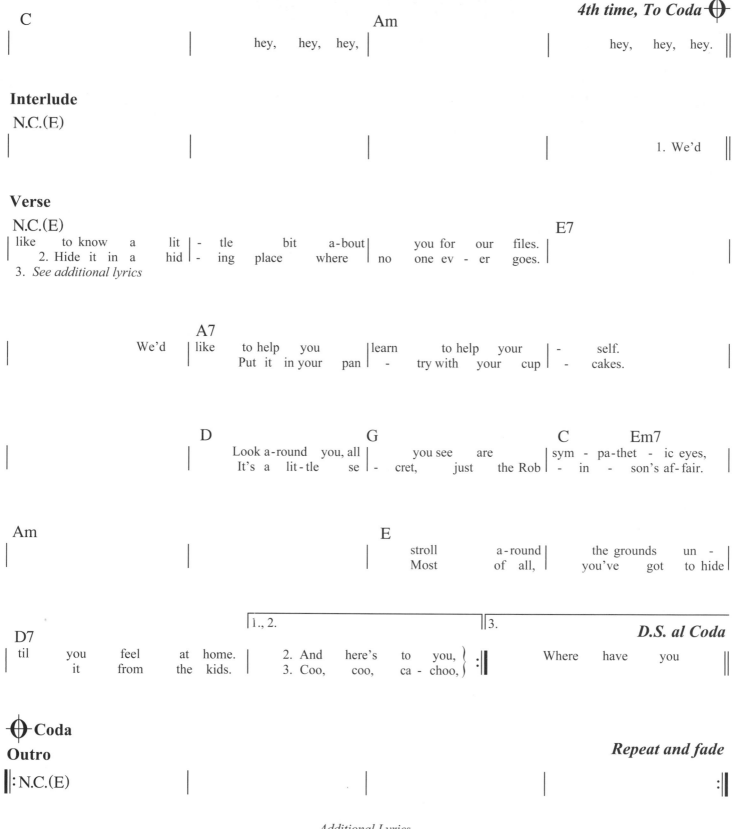

C　　　　　　　　　　　　　　　　　　　　　　**Am**

| | | hey,　hey,　hey, | | | hey,　hey,　hey. ‖

Interlude

N.C.(E)

| | | | | 1. We'd ‖

Verse

N.C.(E)　　　　　　　　　　　　　　　　　　　　　　　　　**E7**

| like　to know　a　lit | - tle　　bit　a-bout | you for　our　files. | |
|　　 2. Hide it in a　hid | - ing　place　where | no　one ev - er　goes. |
　3. *See additional lyrics*

　　　　　　　　　　　　　A7

| | We'd | like　to help　you | learn　　to help　your | - self. | |
| | Put it in your　pan | - try with　your　cup | - cakes. |

　　　　　　　　　　　　D　　　　　　**G**　　　　　　　　**C**　　**Em7**

| | | Look a-round　you, all | you see　are | sym - pa-thet - ic eyes, | |
| | It's a　lit-tle　se | - cret,　just　the Rob | - in - son's af-fair. |

Am　　　　　　　　　　　　　　　**E**

| | | stroll　　a-round | the grounds　un - | |
| | Most　　of all, | you've　got　to hide |

　　　　　　　　　　　‖1., 2.　　　　　　　　　　　‖3.　　　　*D.S. al Coda*

D7

| til　you　feel　at home. | 2. And　here's　to　you, ‌}:‖ | Where　have　you | ‖
| it　from　the kids. | 3. Coo,　coo,　ca - choo, |

⊕ **Coda**

Outro　　　　　　　　　　　　　　　　　　　　　　*Repeat and fade*

‖: N.C.(E) | | | :‖

Additional Lyrics

3. Sitting on a sofa on a Sunday afternoon,
　Going to the candidates' debate.
　Laugh about it, shout about it, when you've got to choose,
　Ev'ry way you look at it, you lose.

Chorus 4 Where have you gone, Joe DiMaggio?
　A nation turns its lonely eyes to you,
　Woo, woo, woo.
　What's that you say, Missus Robinson?
　Joltin' Joe has left and gone away,
　Hey, hey, hey,
　Hey, hey, hey.

Morning Has Broken

Words by Eleanor Farjeon
Music by Cat Stevens

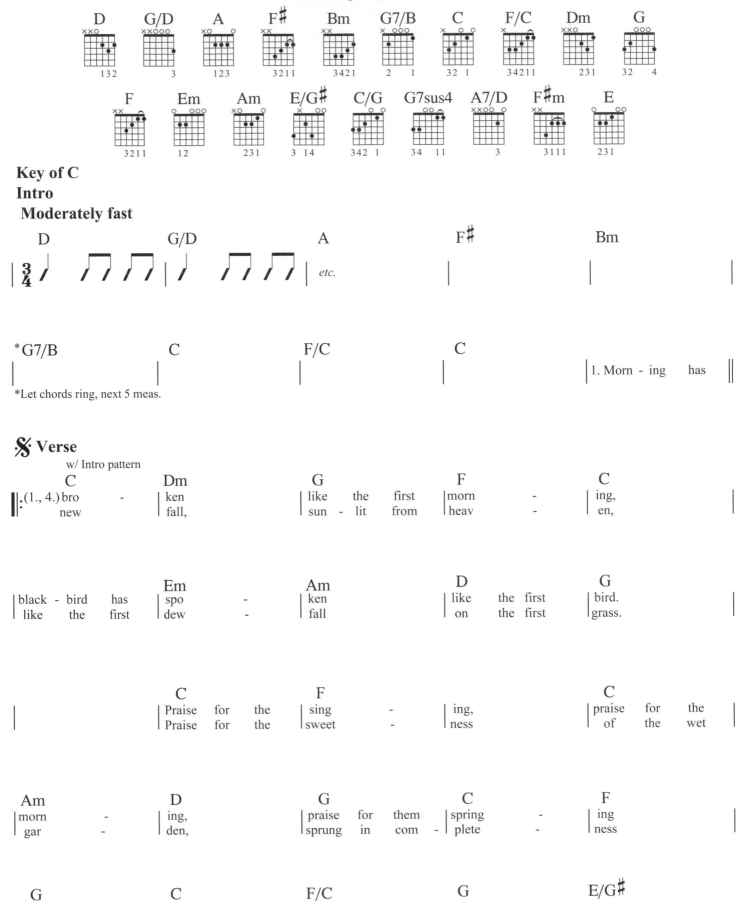

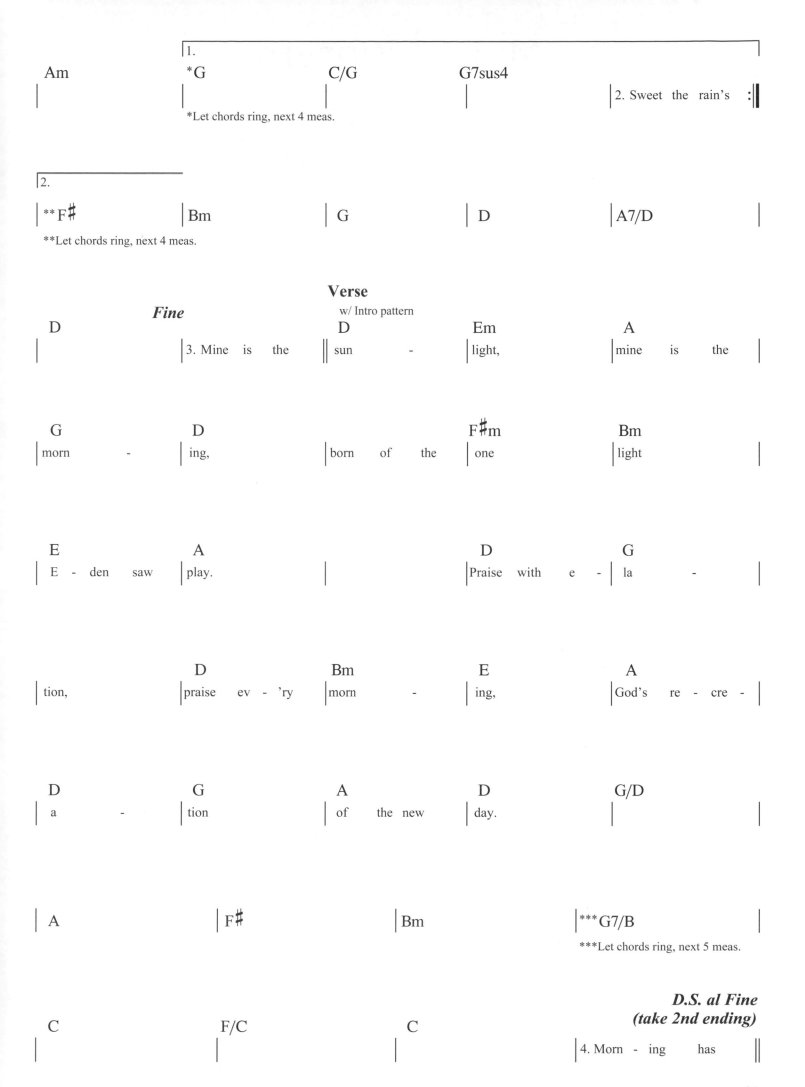

61

Mull of Kintyre

Words and Music by Paul McCartney and Denny Laine

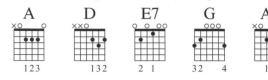

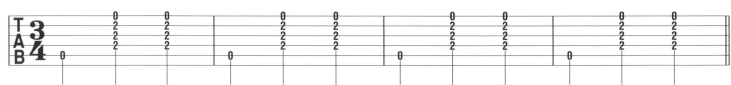

Key of A

Intro

Moderately slow (♫ = ♩♪)

A

```
T  3  |----0-------0-----|------0-------0------|------0-------0-----|------0-------0------|
A  3  |-2--2----2--2-----|---2--2----2--2-----|---2--2----2--2----|---2--2----2--2-----|
B  4  |-2--2----2--2-----|---2--2----2--2-----|---2--2----2--2----|---2--2----2--2-----|
      |-0---------2------|-0--------2---------|-0--------2--------|-0--------2---------|
```

Chorus

A   D
etc.
|Mull   of Kin - |tyre,   oh, |mist roll - ing in | from   the sea. |

A   D
| My de - |sire   is |al - ways   to be | here.   Oh, |

A
|Mull   of Kin - |tyre. | | ‖

𝄋 Verse

A
|1. Far have   I |trav - elled   and |much have   I   seen: | |
|3. Smiles   in the |sun - shine   and |tears   in   the rain |

D   A
|dark   dis - tant moun |- tains   with |val - leys   of |green, |
|still   take   me back | where my |mem'ries   re - |main. |

|past   paint - ed |des - erts,   the |sun - sets   on fire   as he car - |
|Flick - er - ing |em - bers   grow |high - er   and |high'r   as   they |

D   E7   *A
|-   ries me home| to   the |Mull   of Kin - |tyre. | ‖
|car - ry me back| to   the |Mull   of Kin - |tyre. |

                                    *Let chord ring.

Chorus

A   D
|Mull   of Kin - |tyre,   oh, |mist roll - ing in | from   the sea. |

A   D
| My de - |sire   is |al - ways   to be | here.   Oh, |

To Coda 1 ⊕

A
|Mull   of Kin - |tyre. | | | ‖

Interlude

‖: D | | G | :‖

| D | | | ‖

Verse

D
| 2. Sweep through the | heath- er, like | deer in the glen. | |

G   D
| Car - ry me back | to the days | I knew then, | |

| Nights when we sang | like a | heav - en - ly | choir of the |

G   A7   *D
| life and the | times of the | Mull of Kin - | tyre. | ‖
                                                    *Let chord ring.

𝄋𝄋 Chorus

D   G
| Mull of Kin - | tyre, oh, | mist roll - ing in | from the sea. |

D   G   *To Coda 2* ⊕
| My de - | sire is | al - ways to be | here. Oh, |

                              Interlude   *2nd time, D.S. al Coda 1*
D   D   A
| Mull of Kin - | tyre. ‖: | | | :‖

⊕ Coda 1   ⊕ Coda 2

D.S.S. al Coda 2
A7   **D
| | ‖ | Mull of Kin - | tyre. | | ‖
                              **Let chord ring.

Outro   *Repeat and fade*

D   A
‖: (La, la, la, | la, | Mull of Kin - | tyre.) :‖

Night Moves

Words and Music by Bob Seger

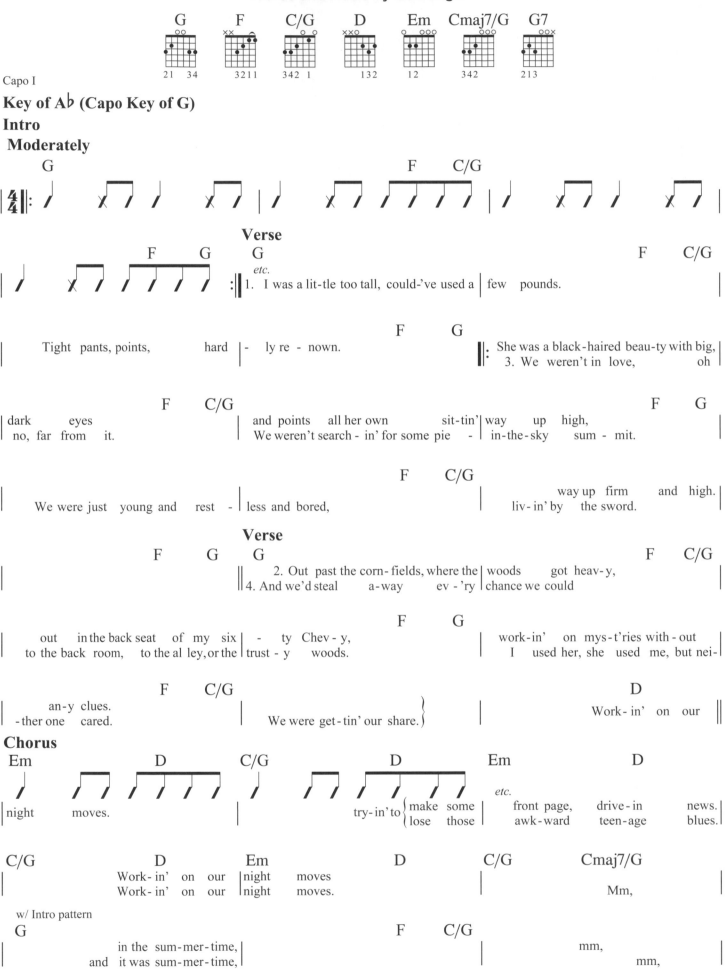

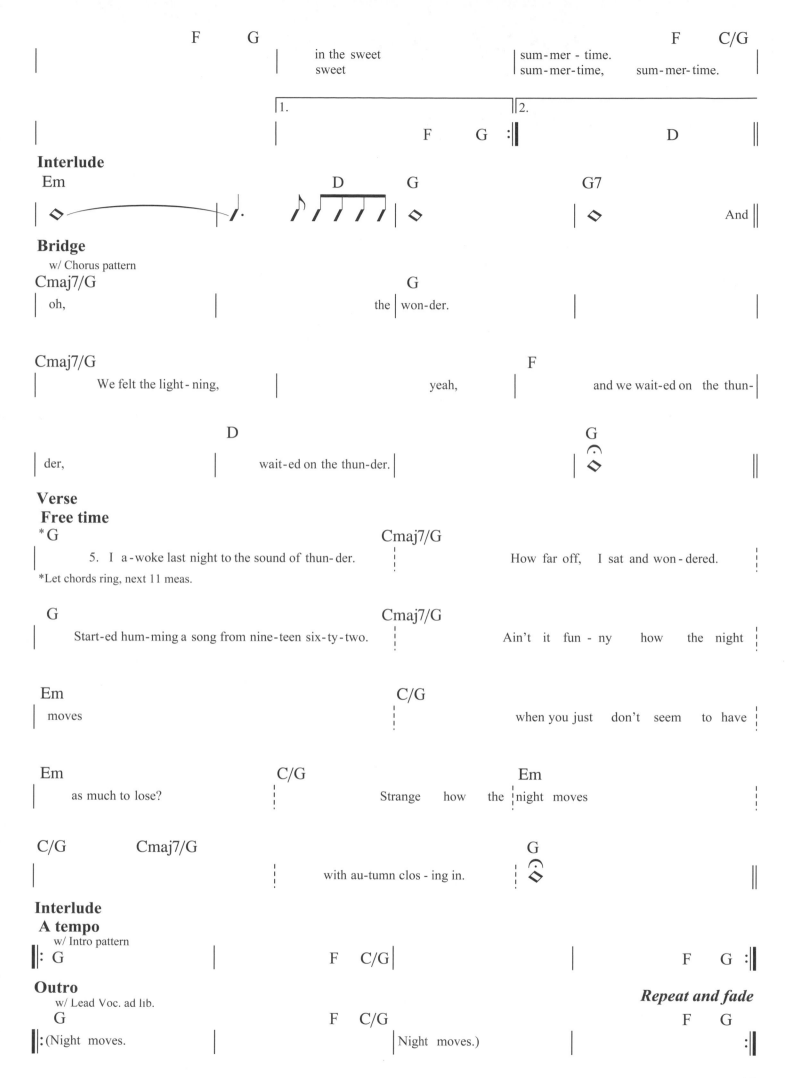

No Woman No Cry

Words and Music by Vincent Ford

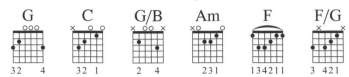

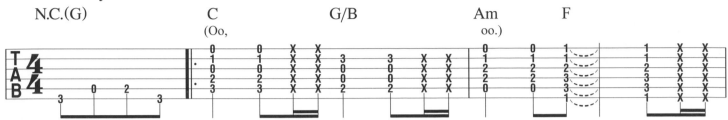

Key of C
Intro
Moderately slow

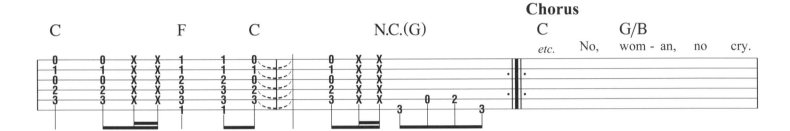

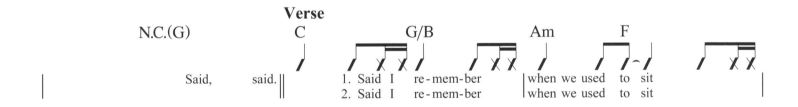

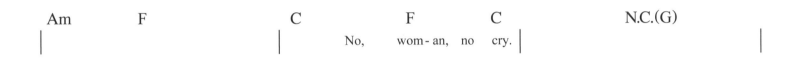

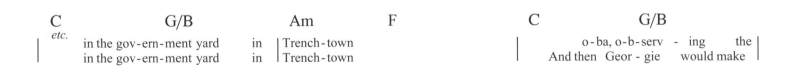

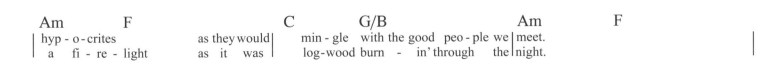

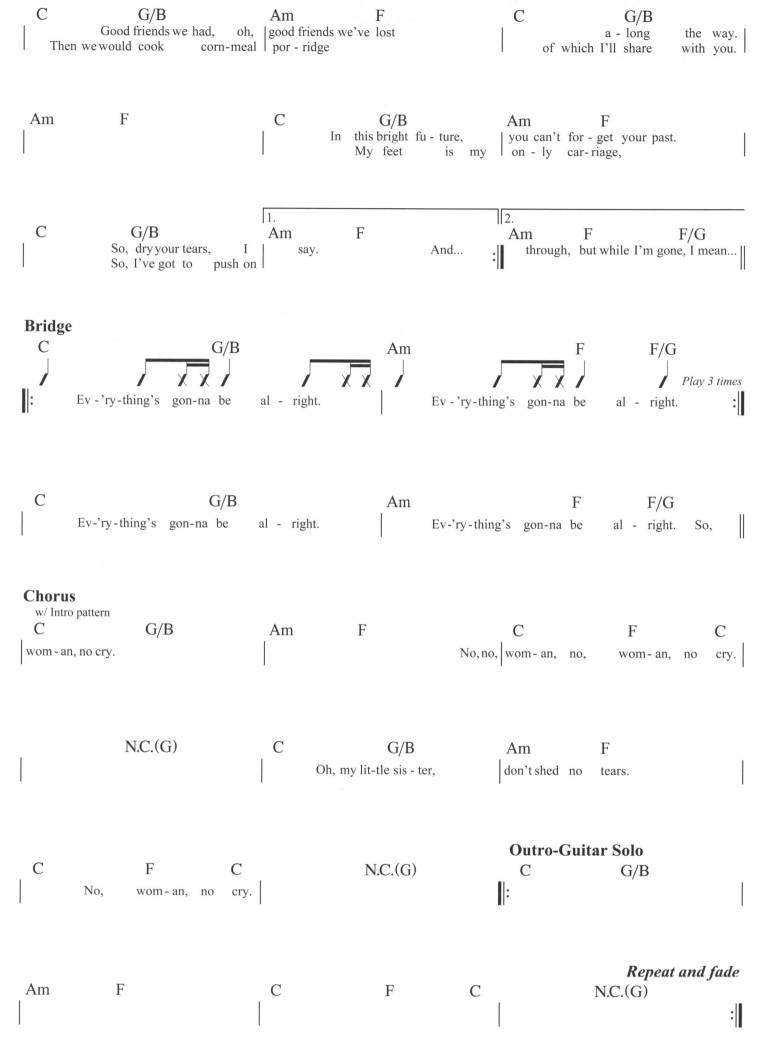

C	G/B	Am	F	C	G/B	
Good friends we had, oh,	good friends we've lost		a - long the way.
Then we would cook corn-meal	por - ridge		of which I'll share with you.

Am	F	C	G/B	Am	F
		In this bright fu - ture,	you can't for - get your past.
		My feet is my	on - ly car - riage,

C	G/B	Am	F	Am	F	F/G
1. So, dry your tears, I	say.	And...	**2.** through, but while I'm gone, I mean...
So, I've got to push on			

Bridge

C ... G/B ... Am ... F ... F/G *Play 3 times*

Ev -'ry-thing's gon-na be al - right. Ev -'ry-thing's gon-na be al - right.

C	G/B	Am	F	F/G
Ev -'ry-thing's gon-na be al - right.		Ev -'ry-thing's gon-na be al - right. So,

Chorus
w/ Intro pattern

C	G/B	Am	F	C	F	C
wom - an, no cry.			No, no,	wom - an, no, wom - an, no cry.

N.C.(G)	C	G/B	Am	F
	Oh, my lit-tle sis - ter,	don't shed no tears.

Outro-Guitar Solo

C	F	C	N.C.(G)	C	G/B
No, wom - an, no cry.			

Repeat and fade

Am	F	C	F	C	N.C.(G)

Patience

Words and Music by W. Axl Rose, Slash, Izzy Stradlin', Duff McKagan and Steven Adler

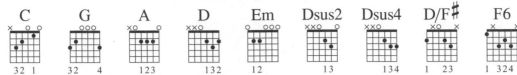

Tune down 1/2 step:
(low to high) Eb-Ab-Db-Gb-Bb-Eb

Key of G
Intro
Moderately

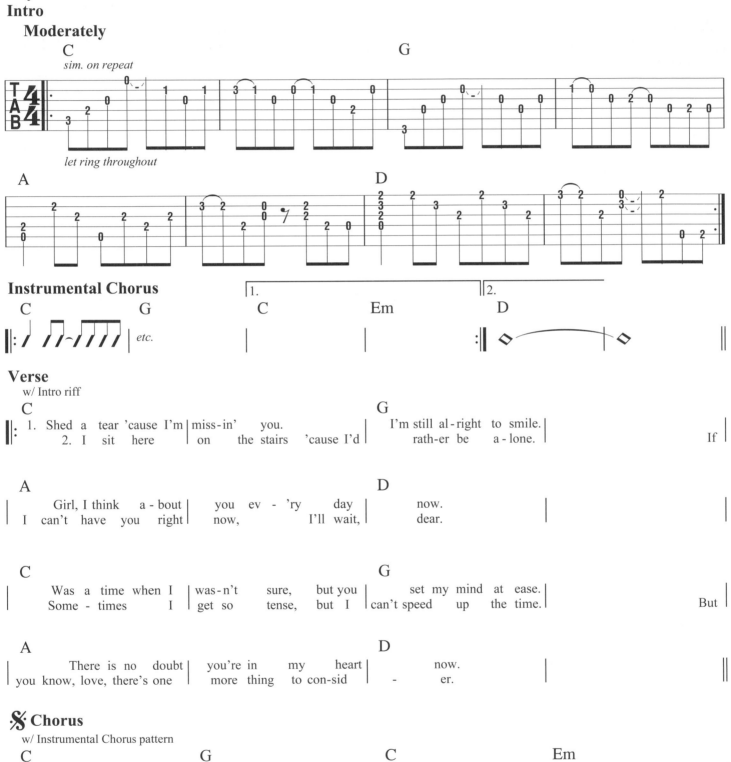

Instrumental Chorus

Verse
w/ Intro riff

C
1. Shed a tear 'cause I'm | miss-in' you.   G I'm still al-right to smile.   If |
2. I sit here | on the stairs 'cause I'd | rath-er be a - lone.

A
Girl, I think a - bout | you ev - 'ry day   D   now. |
I can't have you right | now,   I'll wait, | dear.

C
Was a time when I | was-n't sure, but you   G   set my mind at ease. |
Some - times I | get so tense, but I | can't speed up the time.   But |

A
There is no doubt | you're in my heart   D   now. |
you know, love, there's one | more thing to con-sid | - er.

Chorus
w/ Instrumental Chorus pattern

C
Said, "Wom-an,   G   take it slow,   it -'ll   C   work it - self out fine.   Em |
Said, "Wom-an,   take it slow,   and | things will be just fine. |
3rd time, Guitar Solo

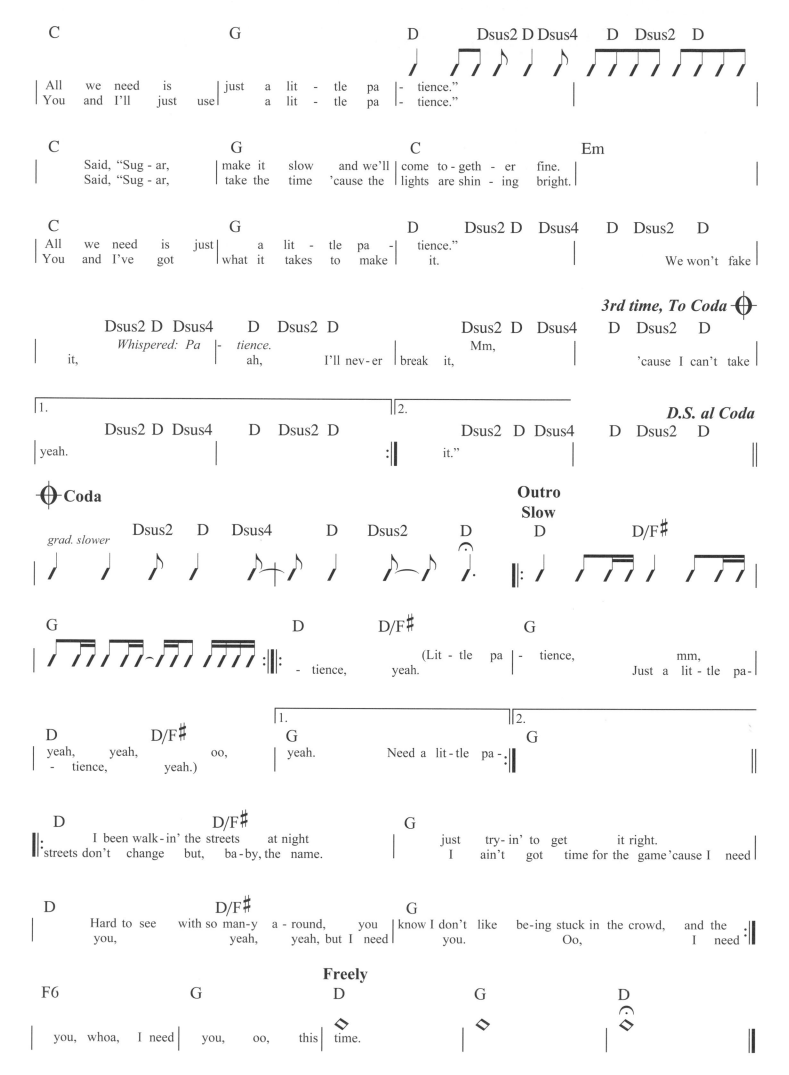

Peaceful Easy Feeling

Words and Music by Jack Tempchin

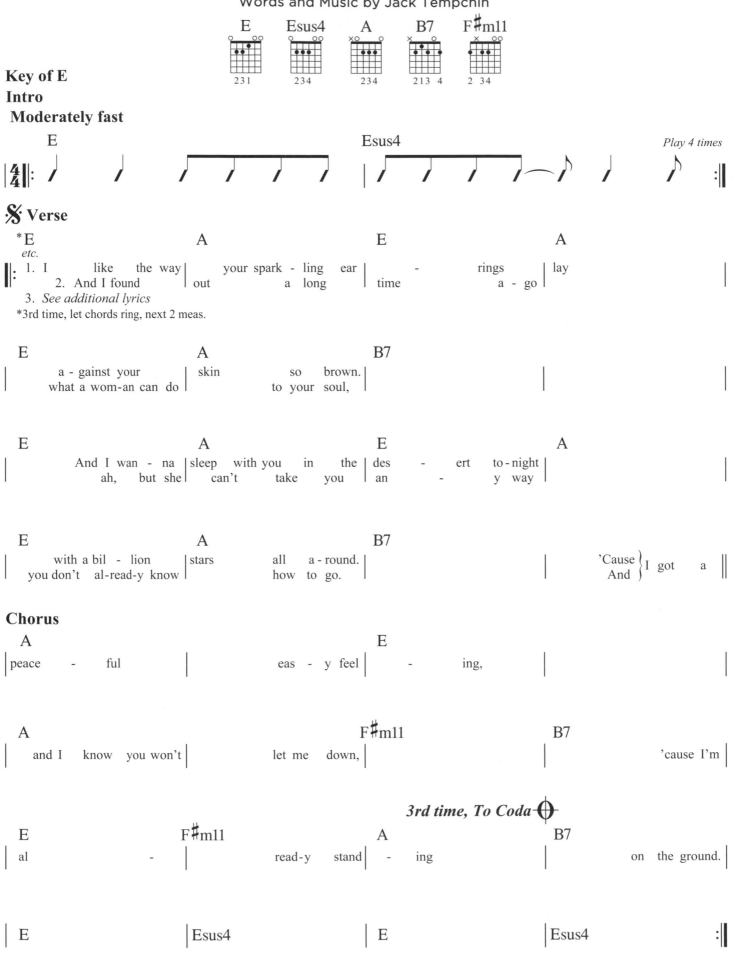

Key of E
Intro
 Moderately fast

Play 4 times

𝄋 Verse

*E   A   E   A
etc.

1. I   like   the   way   your spark - ling   ear   -   rings   lay
2. And I found   out   a   long   time   a - go
3. *See additional lyrics*

*3rd time, let chords ring, next 2 meas.

E   A   B7

a - gainst your   skin   so   brown.
what a wom-an can do   to   your   soul,

E   A   E   A

And I wan - na   sleep   with   you   in   the   des   -   ert to-night
ah, but she   can't   take   you   an   -   y   way

E   A   B7

with a bil - lion   stars   all   a - round.   'Cause ⎰ I got   a
you don't al-read-y know   how   to   go.   And ⎱

Chorus

A   E

peace - ful   eas - y feel   -   ing,

A   F#m11   B7

and I   know   you won't   let   me   down,   'cause I'm

3rd time, To Coda ⊕

E   F#m11   A   B7

al   -   read-y stand   -   ing   on   the   ground.

E   Esus4   E   Esus4

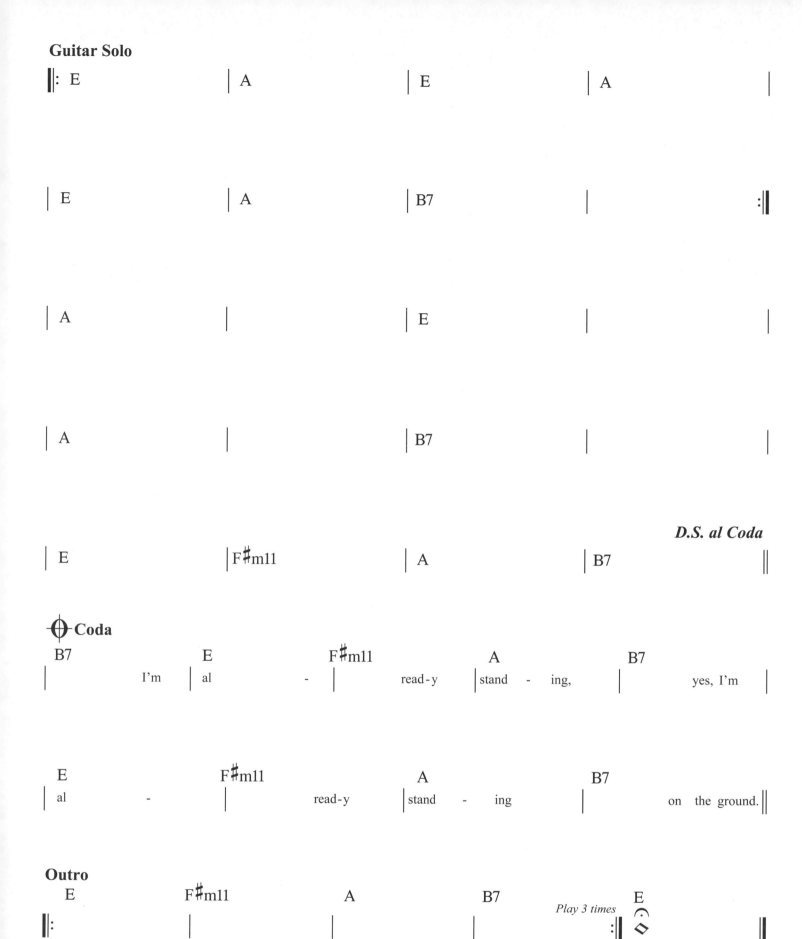

Guitar Solo

‖: E | A | E | A |

| E | A | B7 | :‖

| A | | E | |

| A | | B7 | |

D.S. al Coda

| E | F#m11 | A | B7 ‖

⊕ Coda

B7   E   F#m11   A   B7

| I'm | al   - | read-y | stand - ing, | yes, I'm |

E   F#m11   A   B7

| al   - | read-y | stand - ing | on the ground. ‖

Outro

E   F#m11   A   B7   *Play 3 times*   E

‖: E | | | :‖ E

Additional Lyrics

3. I get this feelin' I may know you
    As a lover and a friend,
    But this voice keeps whispering in my other ear,
    Tells me I may never see you again.
    'Cause I get a…

Photograph

Lyrics by Chad Kroeger
Music by Nickelback

Tune down 1/2 step:
(low to high) Eb-Ab-Db-Gb-Bb-Eb

Key of E

Verse

Slow

E5   Badd4   D⁶₉   Aadd9   G6   Cmaj7

E5   **Badd4**

1. Look at this pho - to - graph,   ev-'ry time I do it makes me laugh.

D⁶₉   **Aadd9**

How did our eyes   get   so   red,   and what the hell is on   Jo-ey's   head?

E5   **Badd4**

etc.

And this is where I   grew   up,   I think the pres-ent own-er fixed   it   up.
2. Re-mem-ber the old ar - cade?   Blew ev-'ry dol-lar that we ev-er   made.

D⁶₉   **Aadd9**

I nev-er knew we ev-er went with - out,   the sec-ond floor is hard for sneak-in' out.
The cops   hat-ed us hang - in' out;   they say some-bod-y went and burned it   down.

E5   **Badd4**

And this is where I   went to school,   most of the time, had bet-ter things   to do.
We used to lis-ten to the ra - di-o   and sing a-long with ev-'ry song we'd   know.

D⁶₉   **Aadd9**

Crim-i - nal rec-ord says I broke in twice,   I must have done it half a doz-en   times.
We said some-day we'd find out how it feels   to sing to more than just the steer-ing wheel.

E5   **Badd4**

I won-der if it's too   late,   should I go back and try to grad - u-ate?
Kim's the first   girl I kissed,   I was so nerv-ous that I near-ly   missed.

D⁶₉   **Aadd9**

Life's bet-ter now then it was back   then,   if I was them I would-n't let me   in.
She's had a cou-ple of kids since   then;   I have-n't seen her since God knows   when.

G6   **Aadd9**

Oh,   whoa,   whoa.   Oh God, I,   I...   Ev-'ry

§ Chorus

E5 ... Badd4
| mem - o - ry of look-ing out the back door, I have a | pho-to al-bum spread out on my bed - room floor. It's |

D$_9^6$ ... Aadd9
| hard to say it, time to say it, | good - bye, good - bye. Ev-'ry |

E5 ... Badd4
| mem-o-ry of walk-ing out the front door. I found the | pho-to of the friend that I was look - ing for. It's |

3rd time, To Coda ⊕ |1.
D$_9^6$ ... Aadd9 ... E5
| hard to say it, time to say it, | good - bye, good - bye. | |

Badd4 ... G6 ... Aadd9
| | | Good - bye. :||

|2.
Aadd9 ... Cmaj7 ... D$_9^6$
| Good - bye, good - bye. | | ||

Bridge

E5 ... Badd4 ... G6
| I miss that town, | I miss their fac | - es. You can't e - rase, |

Aadd9 ... E5 ... Badd4
| you can't re - place | it. I miss it now, | I can't be - lieve |

G6 ... Aadd9 ... **Verse** E5
| it. So hard to stay, | too hard to leave || it. 3. If I could re - live those days, |

Badd4 ... D$_9^6$ ... *D.S. al Coda*
| I know the one thing that would nev - er change. | Ev-'ry ||

⊕ Coda ... **Outro-Verse**

Aadd9 ... E5
| good - bye, good - bye. || Look at this pho - to - graph, |

Badd4 ... D$_9^6$ ... Aadd9
| ev - 'ry time I do, it makes me laugh. | Ev-'ry time I do, it makes me... | ||

Pink Houses

Words and Music by John Mellencamp

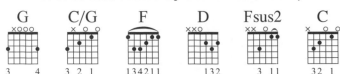

Key of G

Intro

Moderately

% Verse

G

| man | | with a black | cat, | | liv - in' in a black neigh-bor-hood. |
| man | | in a tee | - shirt, | | lis-t'nin' to a rock 'n' roll-er |

3. *See additional lyrics*

| sta - tion. | He's got an | in - ter - state run-ning through | his front yard, and you know he thinks |
| | He's got a | greas-y hair and a | greas-y smile. He says, "Lord, |

F   C/G   G

| he's | got it so good. | | And there's a wom- |
| this must be | my des - ti - na | - tion." | 'Cause they told |

| - an | in the kitch | - en, | clean - ing up the eve - ning slop. |
| me | when I was youn | - ger, | say - in', "Boy, you're gon - na be pres-i-dent." |

| | And he looks | at her and says "Hey dar - lin', | I can re-mem-ber when you could |
| | But just like | ev - 'ry - thing else, those old cra - | zy dreams just kind of came and |

Chorus

G   C/G

| stop a clock." } | Oh, but ain't that A - mer - | i - ca, for you and me. |
| went. | | |

G   C/G   G

| Ain't that A - mer-i | - ca, some-thing to see, | ba - by. Ain't that A - mer- |

3rd time, To Coda ⊕

C/G   D

| i - ca, home of the free, | yeah. | Lit - tle pink hous - es for |

Interlude
w/ Intro riff

C/G
| you and me.   { Oh, | yeah,   for you and me.   N.C.   G
                 { Oh, | build them ba - by, for || you and me.   Ow. |

| 1. | 2.
C/G   G   N.C.   G   C/G   G   C/G   G   N.C.
| | | 2. Well, there's a young :|| |

Bridge

| G |C/G   G   N.C. ||: Fsus2 | C |

G   *Play 4 times*   ***D.S. al Coda***
| | :|| | 3. Well, there's peo -||

✵ Coda

C/G   G
| you and me.   Ooh. | | Ooh, yeah!| Oh, ain't that A - mer -|

C/G   G   C/G
| i - ca,   for you and   me. | Ain't that A - mer -i |- ca,   some - thing to   see, |

G   C/G   D
| ba - by. Ain't that A - mer -| i - ca,   home of the free,| Ooh, yeah, |

                              C/G   N.C.
| yeah,   yeah, yeah, yeah,   yeah, | yeah.   Lit-tle pink hous -| es babe,   for you and   me. ||

Outro
w/ Intro riff
                              | 1., 2., 3. | 4.
G   C/G   G   N.C.   C/G   G
||: | :|| /.   ♪ ♩ 𝄐 ||

See additional lyrics

3. Well, there's people, and more people,
   And what do they know, know, know?
   Go to work in some high-rise
   And vacation down at the Gulf of Mexico, ooh, yeah.
   And there's winners and there's losers,
   But they ain't no big deal.
   'Cause the simple man, baby,
   Pays for the thrills, the bills, the pills that kill.

Rocky Mountain High

Words and Music by John Denver and Mike Taylor

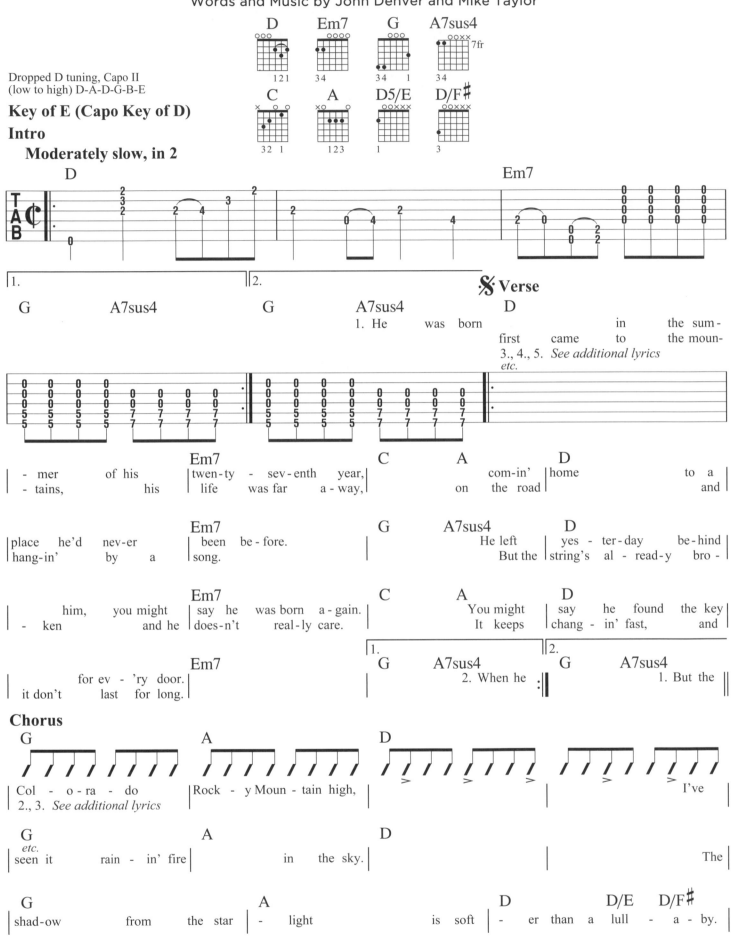

Dropped D tuning, Capo II
(low to high) D-A-D-G-B-E

Key of E (Capo Key of D)

Intro

Moderately slow, in 2

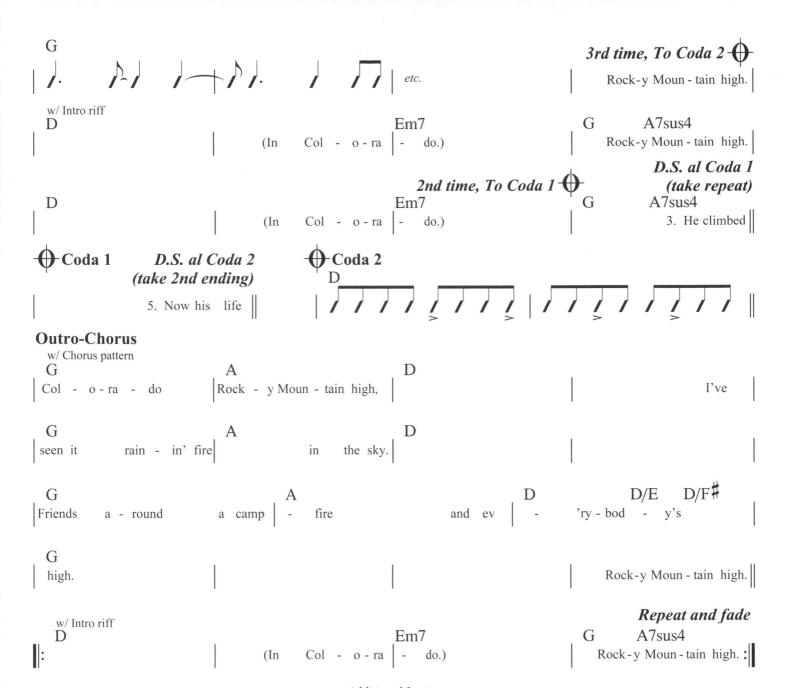

Additional Lyrics

3. He climbed cathedral mountains, he saw silver clouds below.
   He saw ev'rything as far as you can see.
   And they say that he got crazy once and he tried to touch the sun,
   And he lost a friend but kept the memory.

4. Now he walks in quiet solitude the forests and the streams,
   Seeking grace in every step he takes.
   His sight has turned inside himself to try and understand
   The serenity of a clear blue mountain lake.

Chorus 2 And the Colorado Rocky Mountain high,
   I've seen it rainin' fire in the sky.
   You can talk to God and listen to the casual reply.
   Rocky Mountain high. (In Colorado.)
   Rocky Mountain high. (In Colorado.)

5. Now his life is full of wonder but his heart still knows some fear
   Of a simple thing he cannot comprehend:
   Why they try to tear the mountains down to bring in a couple more,
   More people, more scars upon the land.

Chorus 3 And the Colorado Rocky Mountain high,
   I've seen it rainin' fire in the sky.
   I know he'd be a poorer man if he never saw an eagle fly.
   Rocky Mountain high.

Runaway Train

Words and Music by David Pirner

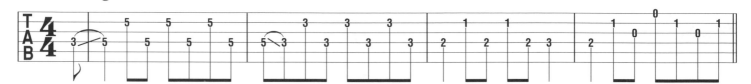

Key of C
Intro
 Moderately

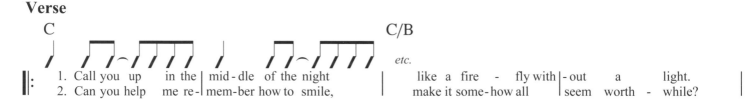

Verse

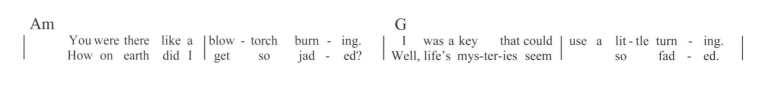

C		**C/B**
1. Call you up in the | mid-dle of the night		like a fire-fly with |-out a light. |
2. Can you help me re-|mem-ber how to smile,		make it some-how all | seem worth-while? |

Am		**G**
You were there like a |blow-torch burn-ing.		I was a key that could | use a lit-tle turn-ing. |
How on earth did I |get so jad-ed?		Well, life's mys-ter-ies seem | so fad-ed. |

C		**C/B**
So tired that I |could-n't e-ven sleep.		So man-y se-crets | I could-n't keep. |
I can go where no | one else can go.		I know what no | one else knows. |

Am		**G**
Prom-ised my-self | I would-n't weep.		A, one more prom-ise | I could-n't keep. It seems‖
Here I am just |drown-in' in the rain		with a tick-et for a |run-a-way train. And ev-‖

Pre-Chorus

F	**G**	**C** **Am**
no one can help| me now. I'm in | too deep, there's no | way out.
-'ry-thing seems cut | and dry. Day | and night, earth| and sky.

F	**Em**	**G**
This time I have | real-ly led my-|self a-stray. | ‖
Some-how I | just don't be-|lieve it. | ‖

𝄋 Chorus

C	**Em**
Run-a-way train, | nev-er go-ing back. | Wrong way on a | one-way track. |

Am	**G**
Seems like I should be | get-ting some-where, | but some-how I'm neith-er |

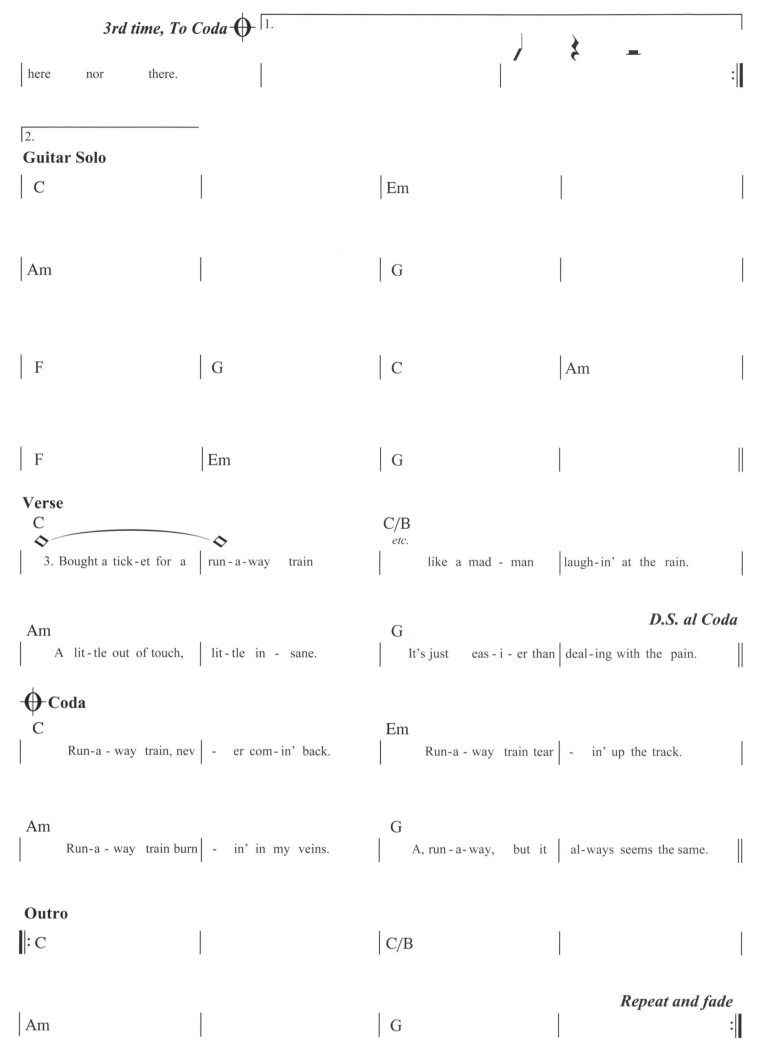

3rd time, To Coda ⊕ |1.

here   nor   there.

|2.

Guitar Solo

| C | | | Em | | |

| Am | | | G | | |

| F | G | | C | Am | |

| F | Em | | G | | |

Verse

C

| 3. Bought a tick-et for a | run-a-way train | C/B *etc.* like a mad-man | laugh-in' at the rain. |

Am

D.S. al Coda

| A lit-tle out of touch, | lit-tle in - sane. | G It's just eas-i-er than | deal-ing with the pain. |

⊕ **Coda**

C

| Run-a-way train, nev - er com-in' back. | Em Run-a-way train tear - in' up the track. |

Am

| Run-a-way train burn - in' in my veins. | G A, run-a-way, but it al-ways seems the same. |

Outro

‖: C | | C/B | |

Repeat and fade

| Am | | G | :‖

The Scientist

Words and Music by Guy Berryman, Jon Buckland, Will Champion and Chris Martin

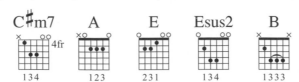

C#m7   A   E   Esus2   B

Capo I

Key of Dm (Capo Key C#m)

Intro

Slow

C#m7 | A | E | Esus2

Verse

C#m7

1. Come up to meet | you, tell you I'm sor | ry, you don't know how love-
2. I was just guess | -ing at num-bers and fig | -ures, pull-ing the puz-

Esus2   C#m7

- ly you are. | I had to find | you, tell you I need
- zles a-part. | Ques-tions of sci | -ence, sci-ence and pro-

E   Esus2   C#m7

you, tell you I'll set | you a-part. | Tell me your se-
- gress do not speak as loud | as my heart. | And tell me you love

A   E   Esus2

- crets and ask me your ques | -tions, oh let's go back | to the start. |
me and come back and haunt | me, oh when I rush | to the start. |

C#m7   A   E   Esus2

Run-ning in cir | -cles, com-ing in tails, | heads are a sci | -ence a-part.
Run-ning in cir | -cles, chas-in' our tails, | com-in' a back | as we are.

Chorus

A   E

| No - bod-y said it was eas - y, | it's such a shame |

Esus2   A   E

| for us to part. | No - bod-y said it was eas - y, | no one ev - er |

                          B

| said it would be { this hard. / so hard. } | Oh, take me back to the start. / I'm go - in' back to the start. ||

Interlude

| E | A | E | |

| C#m7 | A | E | Esus2 :|| [1.] [2.] ||

Outro

C#m7   A   E   *Play 3 times*

||: Ah, oo, | oo, oo, oo, | oo. | :||

C#m7   A   E

| Ah, oo, | oo, oo, oo, | oo. ||

81

She Talks to Angels

Words and Music by Chris Robinson and Rich Robinson

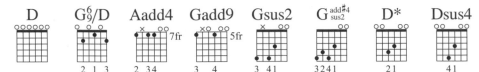

Open D tuning, capo II:
(low to high) D-A-D-F#-A-D

Key of E (Capo Key of D)

Intro

Moderately slow

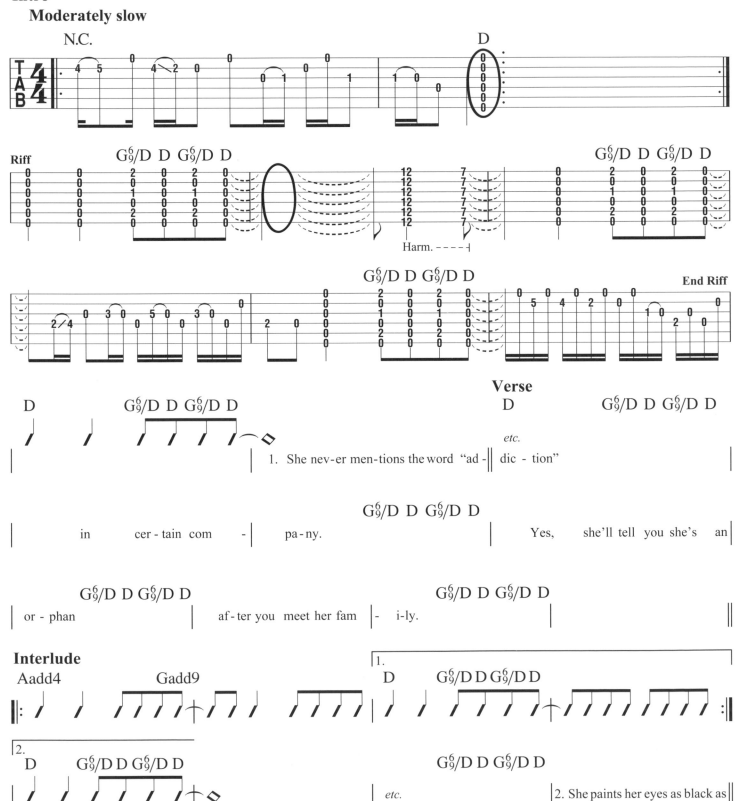

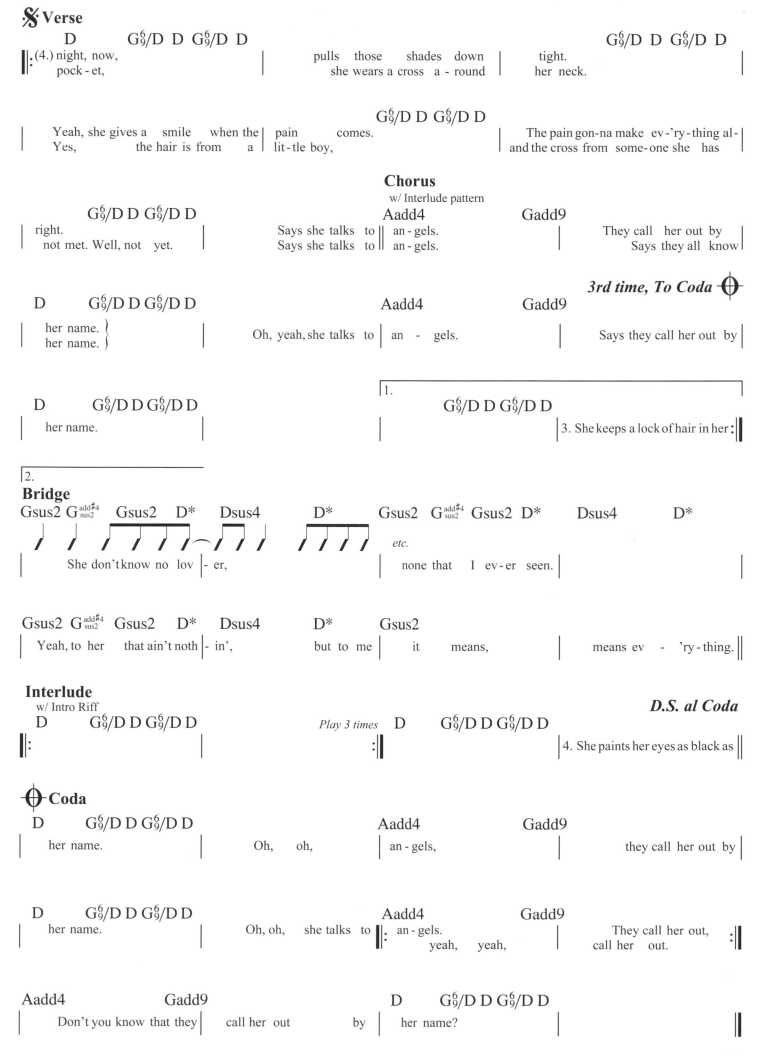

Southern Cross

Words and Music by Stephen Stills, Richard Curtis and Michael Curtis

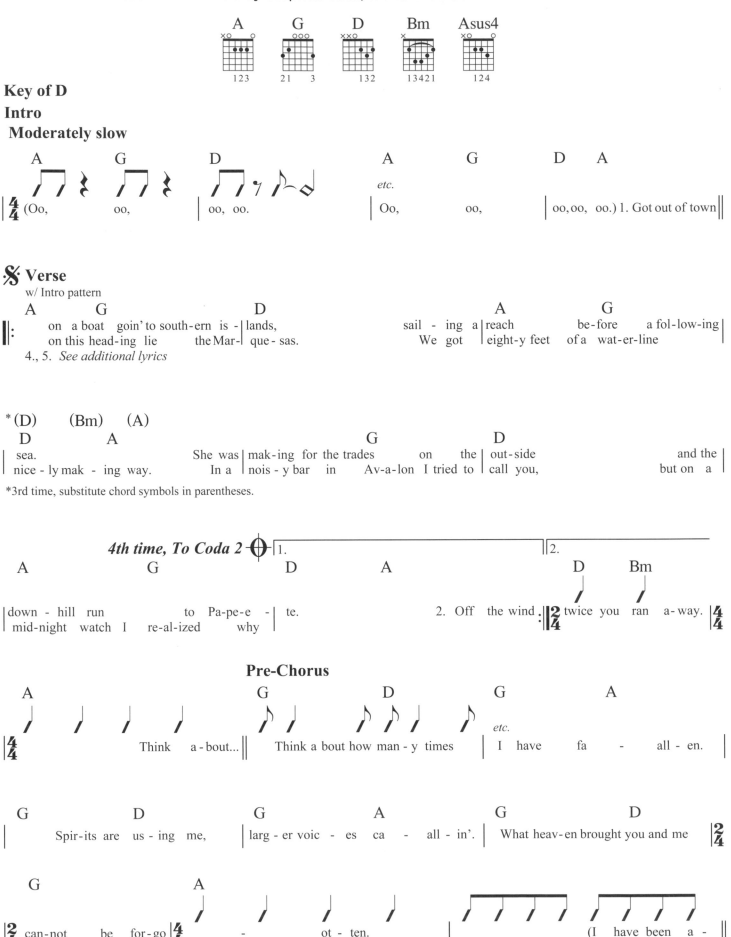

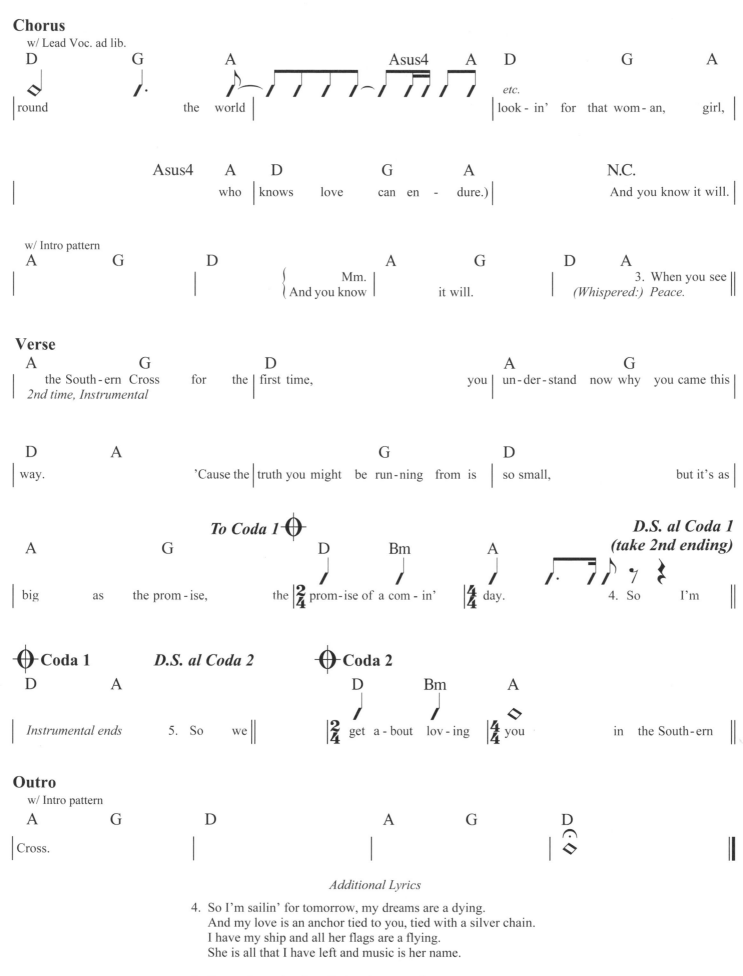

Additional Lyrics

4. So I'm sailin' for tomorrow, my dreams are a dying.
   And my love is an anchor tied to you, tied with a silver chain.
   I have my ship and all her flags are a flying.
   She is all that I have left and music is her name.

5. So we cheated and we lied and we tested.
   And we never failed to fail; it was the easiest thing to do.
   You will survive being bested.
   Somebody fine will come along, make me forget about loving you
   In the Southern Cross.

Sweet Caroline

Words and Music by Neil Diamond

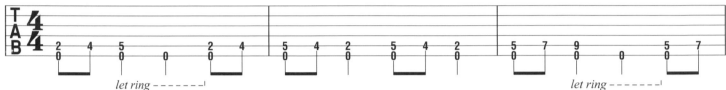

Capo II

Key of B (Capo Key of A)

Intro

Moderately fast (♫ = ♪♪)

N.C.(E5)

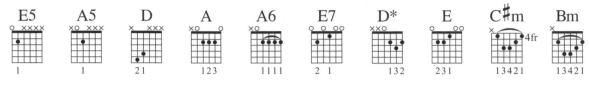

let ring - - - - - - -

let ring - - - - - - -

let ring - - - -

Verse

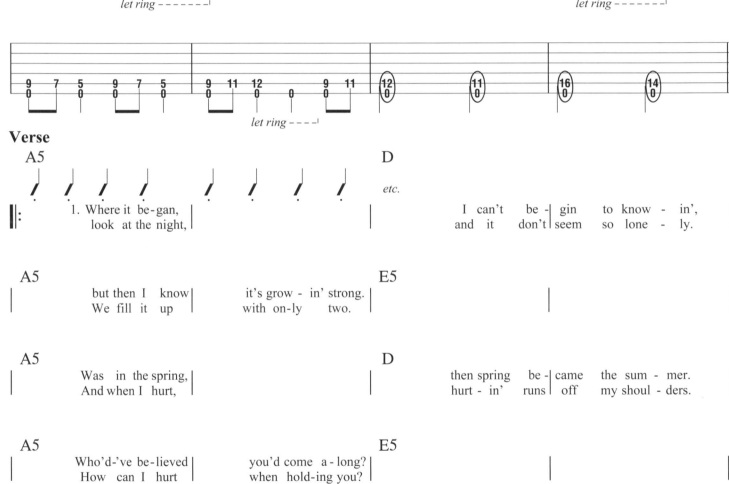

A5   D

etc.

1. Where it be-gan,   I can't be-|gin to know - in',
look at the night,   and it don't| seem so lone - ly.

A5   E5

but then I know| it's grow - in' strong.
We fill it up| with on-ly two.

A5   D

Was in the spring,| then spring be-|came the sum - mer.
And when I hurt,| hurt - in' runs| off my shoul - ders.

A5   E5

Who'd-'ve be-lieved| you'd come a - long?
How can I hurt| when hold-ing you?

Pre-Chorus

A   A6

etc.

Hands   touch-ing hands, }
Warm   touch-ing warm, }

E7   D*

reach-ing out,   touch-ing me,   touch - ing

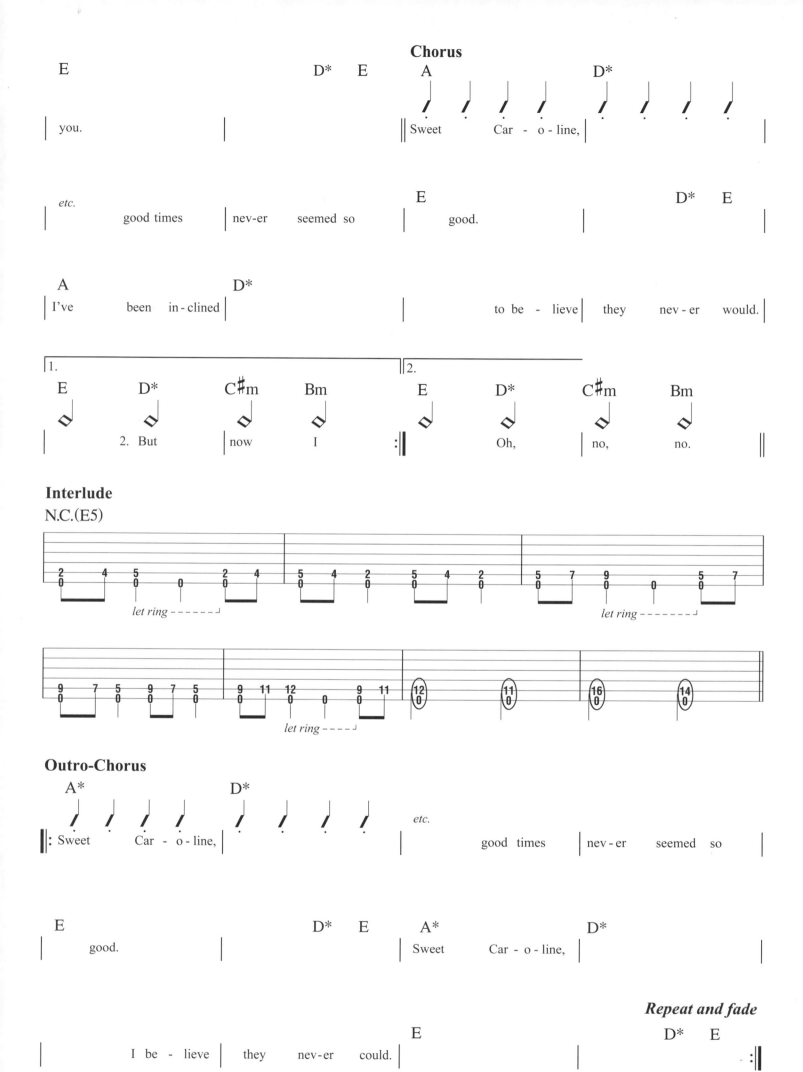

Teardrops on My Guitar

Words and Music by Taylor Swift and Liz Rose

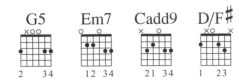

Capo III

Key of B♭ (Capo Key of G)

Intro

Moderately

Half-time feel

G5 Em7 Cadd9 D/F#

Verse

pick chords

G5	Em7	Cadd9
1. Drew looks	at me,	I fake

D/F#	G5	Em7
a smile so he won't see	that I want	and I'm need-

Cadd9	D/F#	**Pre-Chorus** Em7 ◇
-in' ev-'ry-thing that we should be.		I'll bet she's beau-ti-ful,

Cadd9	G5	D/F#
etc. that girl he talks a-bout.	And she's got ev-'ry-thing that	I have to live with-out.

Verse

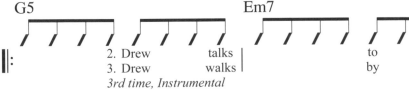

G5	Em7	Cadd9
2. Drew talks 3. Drew walks *3rd time, Instrumental*	to me, by me,	*etc.* I laugh can

D/F#	G5	Em7
'cause it's just so fun-ny he tell that I can't breathe?	that I can't And there he goes,	e-ven see so per-fect-ly,

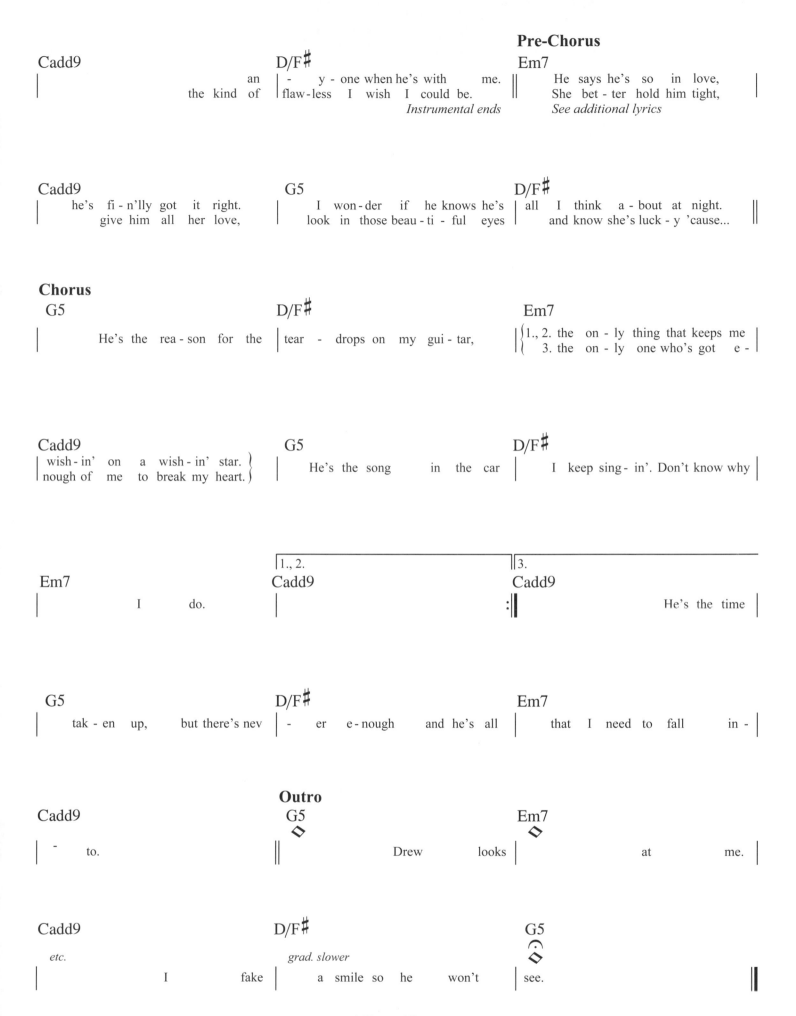

Pre-Chorus

Cadd9   D/F♯   Em7

an | - y - one when he's with me. ‖ He says he's so in love,
the kind of | flaw-less I wish I could be. ‖ She bet - ter hold him tight,
Instrumental ends   *See additional lyrics*

Cadd9   G5   D/F♯

he's fi - n'lly got it right. | I won - der if he knows he's | all I think a - bout at night. ‖
give him all her love, | look in those beau - ti - ful eyes | and know she's luck - y 'cause...

Chorus

G5   D/F♯   Em7

He's the rea - son for the | tear - drops on my gui - tar, | 1., 2. the on - ly thing that keeps me
                                                   3. the on - ly one who's got e -

Cadd9   G5   D/F♯

wish - in' on a wish - in' star. | He's the song in the car | I keep sing - in'. Don't know why
nough of me to break my heart.

Em7   ‖1., 2. Cadd9   ‖3. Cadd9

I do. | | : ‖ He's the time

G5   D/F♯   Em7

tak - en up, but there's nev | - er e - nough and he's all | that I need to fall in -

Outro

Cadd9   G5   Em7

- to. ‖ Drew looks | at me.

Cadd9   D/F♯   G5

etc.   *grad. slower*

I fake | a smile so he won't | see. ‖

Additional Lyrics

Pre-Chorus So, I drive home alone. As I turn out the light,
I'll put his picture down and maybe get some sleep tonight 'cause...

To Be with You

Words and Music by Eric Martin and David Grahame

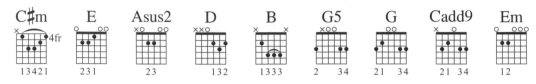

Key of E
Verse
Moderately fast

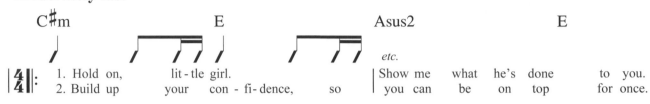

C#m		E		Asus2		E	
1. Hold on,	lit-tle girl.			Show me	what he's done	to you.	
2. Build up	your con-fi-dence, so			you can	be on top	for once.	

C#m		E		Asus2		E	
Stand up,	lit-tle girl.		A	bro-ken heart can't be that bad.		When	
Wake up,	who cares a-bout			lit-tle boys that talk too much.		I	

Asus2		E		Asus2		E		
it's through,	it's through.			Fate will twist the both of you.			So	
seen it all	go down.		Your	game of love was all rained out.				

D		B	
come on ba - by, come on o - ver.		Let me be the one to {show / hold} you.	

𝄋 Chorus

E		Asus2		B		E	
I'm the one who wants to				be with you.			

	Asus2		B		E		Asus2	
Deep in - side I hope you				feel it too.			Wait - ed on a line of	

3rd time, To Coda ⊕

B	*E	(E)	Asus2	B	E	
greens and blues		just to be the next to		be with you.		

*3rd time, substitute C#m.

Bridge

Asus2   C♯m

| Why be a-lone when we can | be to-geth - er, ba - by? |

G5

| You can make my life worth-while. | I can make you start to ‖

Guitar Solo

E   Asus2   B   E   Asus2   B   E

| smile. |

Asus2   B   C♯m   E   Asus2   B   E

3. When ‖

Verse

Asus2   E   Asus2   E

| it's through, it's through. | Fate will twist the both of you. So |

D   B

                                     grad. slower

| come on ba - by, come on o - ver. | Let me be the one to show you. ‖

Chorus

A tempo

G   Cadd9   D   G

| I'm the one who wants to | be with you. |

           Cadd9   D   G   Cadd9

| Deep in-side I hope you | feel it too. | Wait-ed on a line of |

                                                 D.S. al Coda

D   Em   G   Cadd9   D   G

| greens and blues | just to be the next to | be with you. ‖

Coda

                   Asus2   B   E

grad. slower

| Just to be the next to | be with you, | oo. ‖

91

Uncle John's Band

Words by Robert Hunter
Music by Jerry Garcia

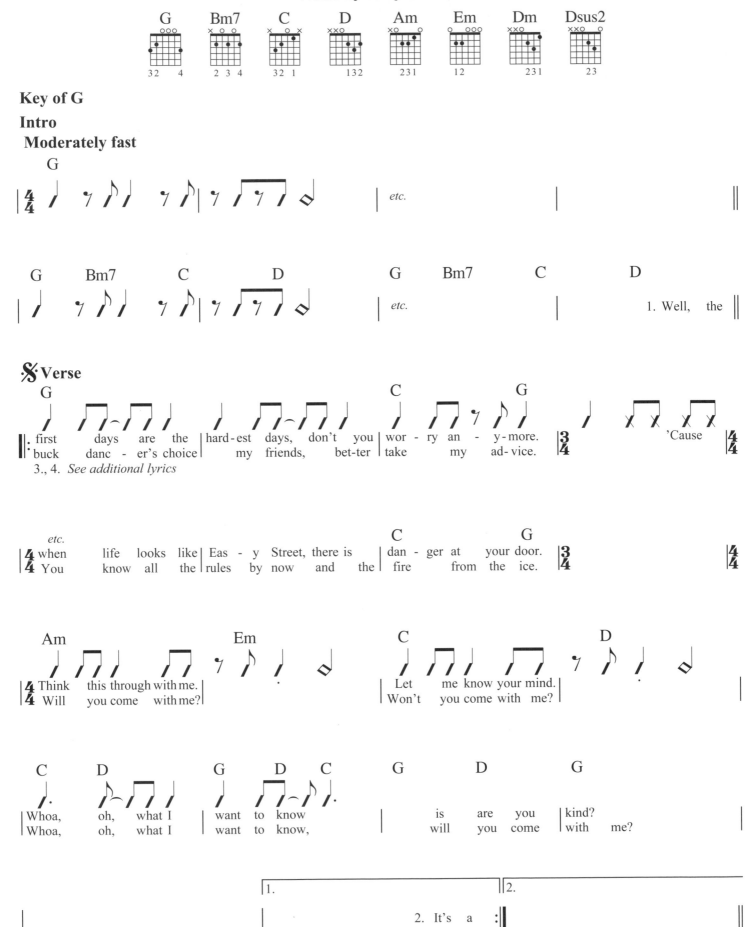

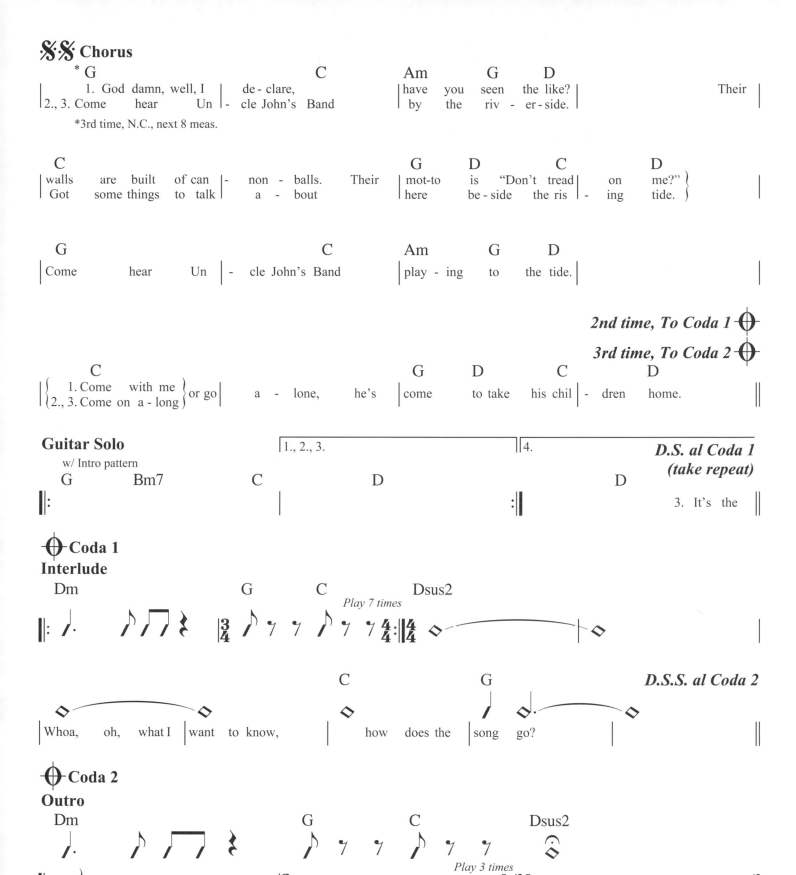

Additional Lyrics

3. It's the same story the crow told me; it's the only one he knows.
Like the morning sun you come and like the wind you go.
Ain't no time to hate, barely time to wait.
Whoa, oh, what I want to know, oh, where does the time go?

4. I live in a silver mine and I call it Beggar's Tomb.
I got me a violin and I beg you call the tune,
Anybody's choice, I can hear your voice.
Whoa, oh, what I want to know, oh, how does the song go?

What's Up

Words and Music by Linda Perry

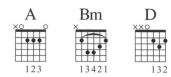

Key of A

Intro

   Slow, in 2

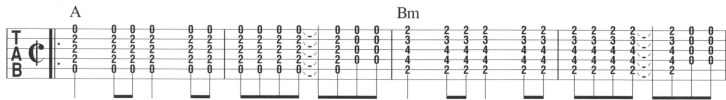

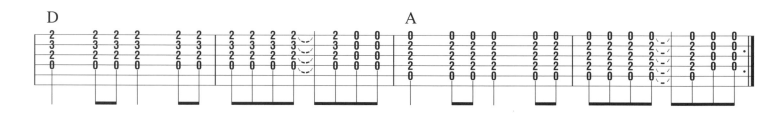

Verse

A   Bm

etc.

| 1. Twen-ty-five years of my | life and   still   I'm | trying   to get up that | great big   hill   of |
| 2. And I try, | oh my God, do   I | try,   I | try   all the |

D   A

| hope | for a des-ti - na |- tion. | I |
| time | in this in-sti - tu |- tion. | And |

| real - ize quick - ly when I | know I should, that the world | was   made up of this | broth-er - hood of |
| I pray, | oh my God,   do I pray, | I | pray ev - 'ry sin-gle |

Bm (above "was made up of this")

D   A

| man, | for what-ev - er that means. | | And so I |
| day | for a rev-o-lu - tion. | | |

Pre-Chorus

A   Bm

| cry some - times when I'm | ly - in' in bed   just to | get it all out, what's in | my   head, and I, |

D   A

| I am feel-ing | a lit-tle pe-cu |- liar. | And so I |

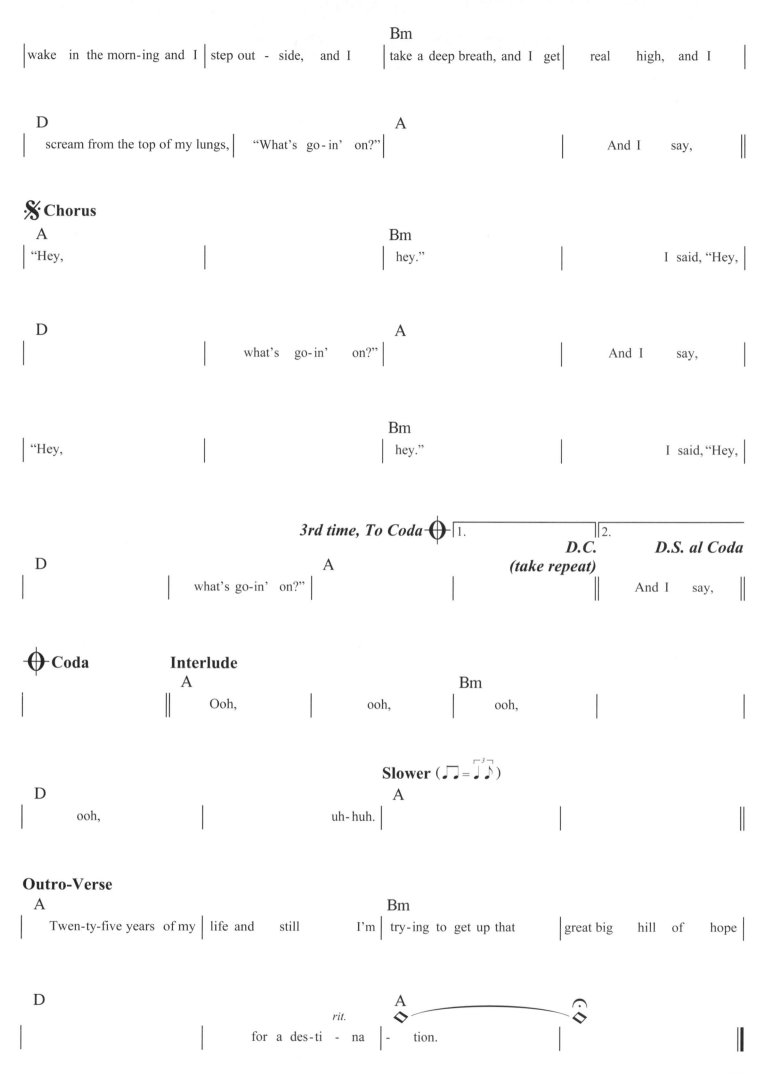

Wonderful Tonight

Words and Music by Eric Clapton

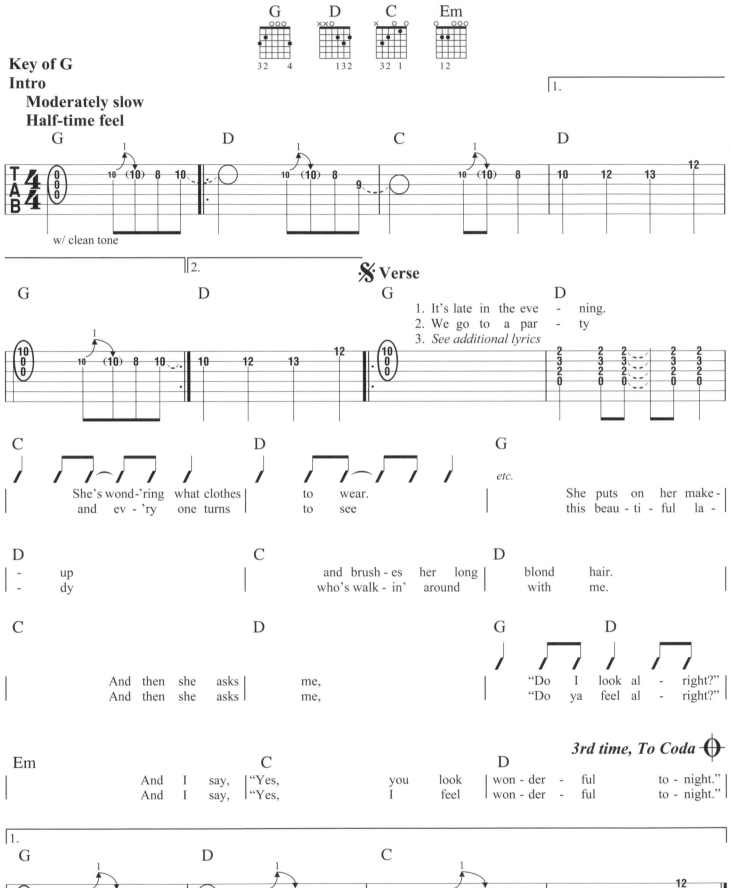

Key of G
Intro
   Moderately slow
   Half-time feel

w/ clean tone

Verse

1. It's late in the eve - ning.
2. We go to a par - ty
3. *See additional lyrics*

She's wond-'ring what clothes to wear.
and ev - 'ry one turns to see

She puts on her make -
this beau - ti - ful la -

- up and brush - es her long blond hair.
- dy who's walk - in' around with me.

And then she asks me,
And then she asks me,

"Do I look al - right?"
"Do ya feel al - right?"

3rd time, To Coda

And I say, "Yes, you look won - der - ful to - night."
And I say, "Yes, I feel won - der - ful to - night."

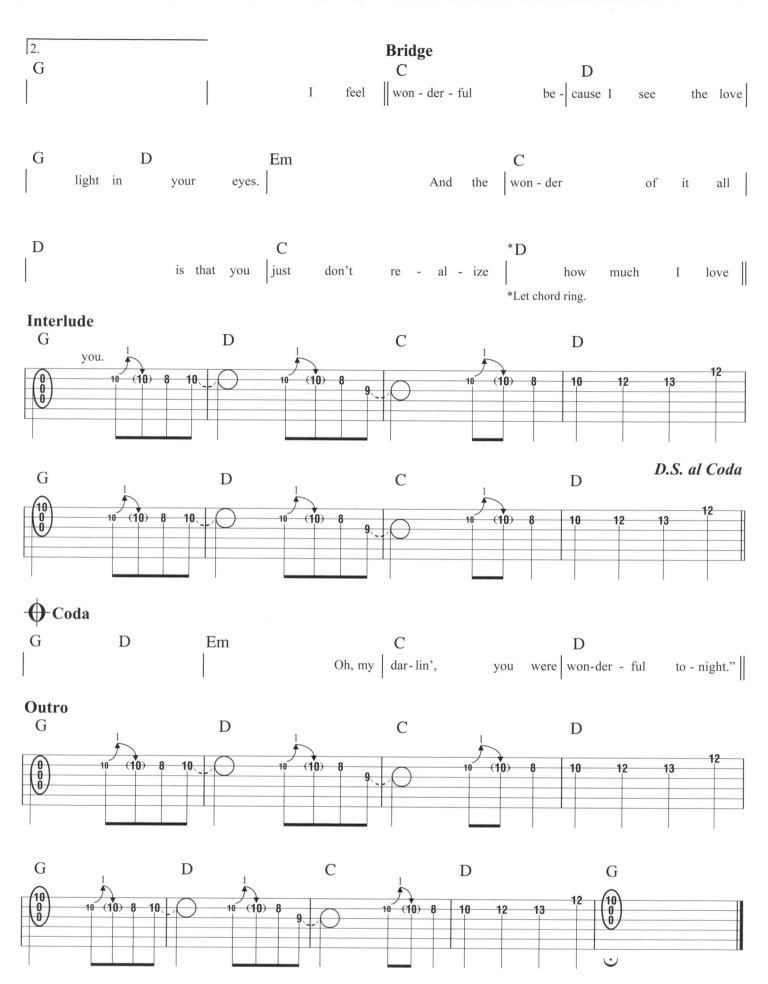

Additional Lyrics

3. It's time to go home now and I've got an aching head.
   So I give her the car keys and she helps me to bed.
   And then I tell her, as I turn out the light,
   I say, "My darlin', you were wonderful tonight.
   Oh, my darlin', you were wonderful tonight."

Wonderwall

Words and Music by Noel Gallagher

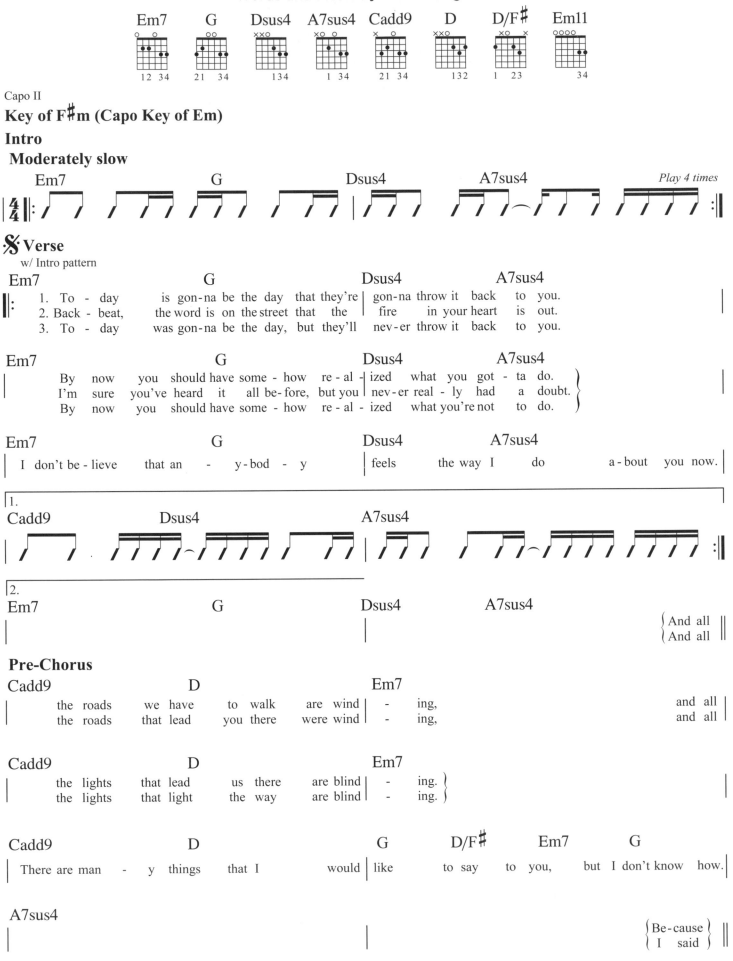

Capo II

Key of F♯m (Capo Key of Em)

Intro

Moderately slow

Verse
w/ Intro pattern

1. To - day   is gon-na be the day   that they're | gon-na throw it back   to you.
2. Back - beat,   the word is on the street that the | fire   in your heart   is out.
3. To - day   was gon-na be the day, but they'll | nev-er throw it back   to you.

By   now   you should have some - how re-al - ized   what you got - ta do.
I'm sure you've heard it   all be-fore, but you | nev-er real - ly had   a doubt.
By   now   you should have some - how re-al - ized   what you're not   to do.

I don't be - lieve   that an - y-bod - y | feels   the way I   do   a-bout you now.

1.

2.
And all
And all

Pre-Chorus

the roads   we have   to walk   are wind | - ing,   and all
the roads   that lead   you there   were wind | - ing,   and all

the lights   that lead   us there   are blind | - ing.
the lights   that light   the way   are blind | - ing.

There are man - y things   that I   would | like   to say   to you,   but I don't know how.

Be-cause
I said

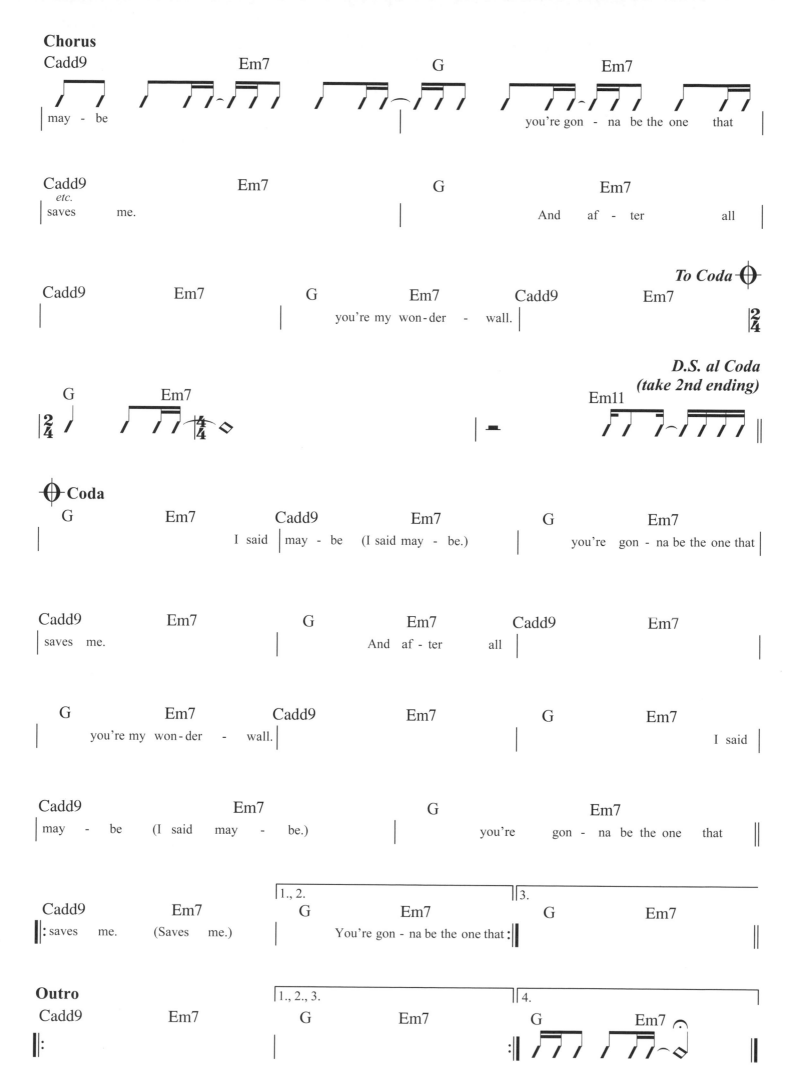

You're Still the One

Words and Music by Shania Twain and R.J. Lange

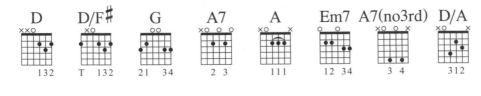

Capo I

Key of E♭ (Capo Key of D)

Intro

Slowly

N.C.
(Drums)

$\frac{4}{4}$

When I first saw you,

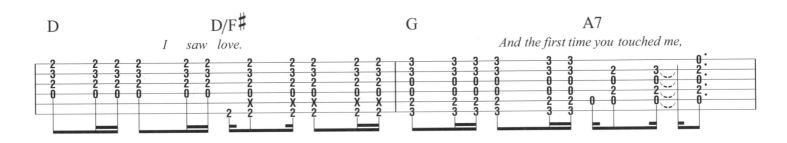

D · · · · · · · · · · · · · · · · · · · D/F♯
I saw love.

G · · · · · · · · · · · · · · · · · · · A7
And the first time you touched me,

D · · · · · · · · · · · · · · · · · · · D/F♯
etc.
I felt love.

G · · · · · · · · · · · · · · · · · · · A7
And after   all this time,

D · · · · · · · · · · · · · · · · · · · D/F♯
you're still   the one I love.   Mm,

G · · · · · · · · · · · · · · · · · · · A7
yeah.

Verse

D · · · · · · · · · · · · · · · · · · · D/F♯
1. Looks   like   we made   it.
2. Ain't   noth - in' bet - ter,

G · · · · · · · · · · · · · · · · · · · A7
Look how   far   we've come,   my ba — by.
we   beat   the odds   to - geth — er.

D · · · · · · · · · · · · · · · · · · · D/F♯
We might a took   the long   way.
I'm glad we did - n't lis - ten.

G · · · · · · · · · · · · · · · · · · · A7
We knew   we'd get   there some - day.}
Look at   what   we would   be miss - ing.}

D · · · · · · · · · · · · · · · · · · · D/F♯
They   said,   "I   bet

G · · · · · · · · · · · · · · · · · · · A7
they'll nev - er make it."   But just

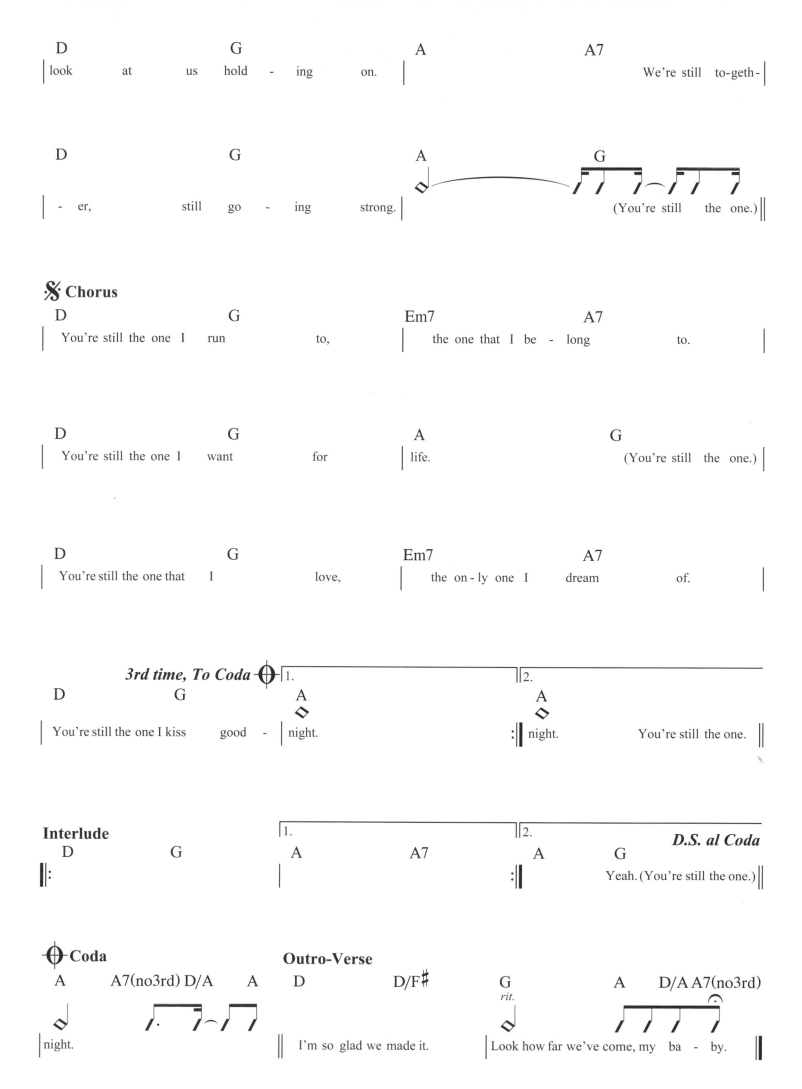

Rhythm Tab Legend

Rhythm Tab is a form of notation that adds rhythmic values to the traditional tab staff.

TABLATURE graphically represents the guitar fingerboard. Each horizontal line represents a string, and each number represents a fret. Rhythmic values are shown using ovals, stems, and dots.

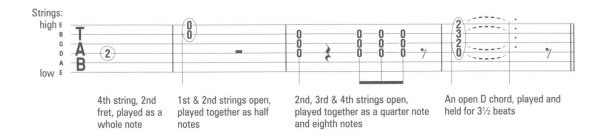

4th string, 2nd fret, played as a whole note

1st & 2nd strings open, played together as half notes

2nd, 3rd & 4th strings open, played together as a quarter note and eighth notes

An open D chord, played and held for 3½ beats

Definitions for Special Guitar Notation

HALF-STEP BEND: Strike the note and bend up 1/2 step.

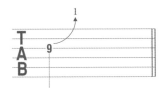

WHOLE-STEP BEND: Strike the note and bend up one step.

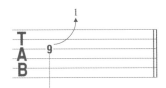

QUARTER-STEP BEND: Strike the note and bend up 1/4 step.

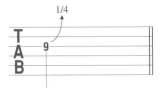

BEND AND RELEASE: Strike the note and bend up as indicated, then release back to the original note. Only the first note is struck.

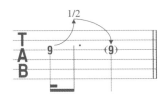

PRE-BEND: Bend the note as indicated, then strike it.

VIBRATO: The string is vibrated by rapidly bending and releasing the note with the fretting hand.

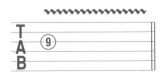

HAMMER-ON: Strike the first (lower) note with one finger, then sound the higher note (on the same string) with another finger by fretting it without picking.

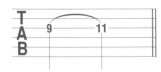

PULL-OFF: Place both fingers on the notes to be sounded. Strike the first note, and without picking, pull the finger off to sound the second (lower) note.

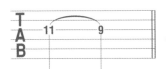

LEGATO SLIDE: Strike the first note and then slide the same fret-hand finger up or down to the second note. The second note is not struck.

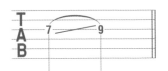

SHIFT SLIDE: Same as legato slide, except the second note is struck.

GRACE-NOTE SLUR: Strike the note and immediately hammer-on (pull-off or slide) as indicated.

TRILL: Very rapidly alternate between the notes indicated by continuously hammering on and pulling off.

NATURAL HARMONIC: Strike the note while the fret hand lightly touches the string directly over the fret indicated.

Harm.

MUFFLED STRINGS: A percussive sound is produced by laying the fret hand across the string(s) without depressing, and striking them with the pick hand.

PALM MUTING: The note is partially muted by the pick hand lightly touching the string(s) just before the bridge.

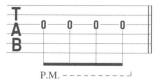

P.M. - - - - - - - -

Additional Musical Definitions

(staccato)	• Play the note short	

Rhy. Fig. • Label used to recall a recurring accompaniment pattern (usually chordal).

Riff • Label used to recall composed, melodic lines (usually single notes) which recur.

(fermata) • A hold or pause

N.C. • No chord

tacet • Instrument is silent (drops out).

⊓ • Downstroke

V • Upstroke

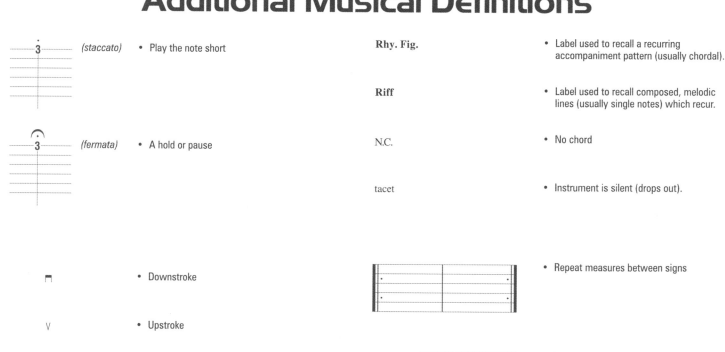

• Repeat measures between signs

1.   2.

• When a repeated section has different endings, play the first ending only the first time and the second ending only the second time.

D.S. al Coda • Go back to the sign (※), then play until the measure marked *"To Coda,"* then skip to the section labelled *"Coda."*

D.C. al Fine • Go back to the beginning of the song and play until the measure marked *"Fine"* (end).

• Repeat previous measure

NOTE: Tablature numbers in parentheses are used when:
  • The note is sustained, but a new articulation begins (such as a hammer-on, pull-off, slide, or bend), or
  • A bend is released.

• Repeat previous two measures

FIRST 50

Books in the First 50 series contain easy to intermediate arrangements for must-know songs.
Each arrangement is simple and streamlined, yet still captures the essence of the tune.

First 50 Baroque Pieces
You Should Play on Guitar

Includes selections by Johann Sebastian Bach, Robert de Visée, Ernst Gottlieb Baron, Santiago de Murcia, Antonio Vivaldi, Sylvius Leopold Weiss, and more.
00322567 ....$14.99

First 50 Bluegrass Solos
You Should Play on Guitar

I Am a Man of Constant Sorrow • Long Journey Home • Molly and Tenbrooks • Old Joe Clark • Rocky Top • Salty Dog Blues • and more.
00298574..$16.99

First 50 Blues Songs
You Should Play on Guitar

All Your Love (I Miss Loving) • Bad to the Bone • Born Under a Bad Sign • Dust My Broom • Hoodoo Man Blues • Little Red Rooster • Love Struck Baby • Pride and Joy • Smoking Gun • Still Got the Blues • The Thrill Is Gone • You Shook Me • and more.
00235790..$17.99

First 50 Blues Turnarounds
You Should Play on Guitar

You'll learn cool turnarounds in the styles of these jazz legends: John Lee Hooker, Robert Johnson, Joe Pass, Jimmy Rogers, Hubert Sumlin, Stevie Ray Vaughan, T-Bone Walker, Muddy Waters, and more.
00277469 ....$14.99

First 50 Chords
You Should Play on Guitar

American Pie • Back in Black • Brown Eyed Girl • Landslide • Let It Be • Riptide • Summer of '69 • Take Me Home, Country Roads • Won't Get Fooled Again • You've Got a Friend • and more.
00300255 Guitar.......................................$12.99

First 50 Classical Pieces
You Should Play on Guitar

Includes compositions by J.S. Bach, Augustin Barrios, Matteo Carcassi, Domenico Scarlatti, Fernando Sor, Francisco Tárrega, Robert de Visée, Antonio Vivaldi and many more.
00155414 ....$16.99

First 50 Folk Songs
You Should Play on Guitar

Amazing Grace • Down by the Riverside • Home on the Range • I've Been Working on the Railroad • Kumbaya • Man of Constant Sorrow • Oh! Susanna • This Little Light of Mine • When the Saints Go Marching In • The Yellow Rose of Texas • and more.
00235868 ....$16.99

First 50 Guitar Duets
You Should Play

Chopsticks • Clocks • Eleanor Rigby • Game of Thrones Theme • Hallelujah • Linus and Lucy (from A Charlie Brown Christmas) • Memory (from Cats) • Over the Rainbow (from The Wizard of Oz) • Star Wars (Main Theme) • What a Wonderful World • You Raise Me Up • and more.
00319706..$14.99

First 50 Jazz Standards
You Should Play on Guitar

All the Things You Are • Body and Soul • Don't Get Around Much Anymore • Fly Me to the Moon (In Other Words) • The Girl from Ipanema (Garota De Ipanema) • I Got Rhythm • Laura • Misty • Night and Day • Satin Summertime • When I Fall in Love • and more.
00198594 Solo Guitar $16.99

First 50 Kids' Songs
You Should Play on Guitar

Do-Re-Mi • Hakuna Matata • Let It Go • My Favorite Things • Puff the Magic Dragon • Take Me Out to the Ball Game • Won't You Be My Neighbor? (It's a Beautiful Day in the Neighborhood) • and more.
00300500 ....$15.99

First 50 Licks
You Should Play on Guitar

Licks presented include the styles of legendary guitarists like Eric Clapton, Buddy Guy, Jimi Hendrix, B.B. King, Randy Rhoads, Carlos Santana, Stevie Ray Vaughan and many more.
00278875 Book/Online Audio..........................$14.99

First 50 Riffs
You Should Play on Guitar

All Right Now • Back in Black • Barracuda • Carry on Wayward Son • Crazy Train • La Grange • Layla • Seven Nation Army • Smoke on the Water • Sunday Bloody Sunday • Sunshine of Your Love • Sweet Home Alabama • Working Man • and more.
00277366 ....$14.99

First 50 Rock Songs You Should
Play on Electric Guitar

All Along the Watchtower • Beat It • Brown Eyed Girl • Cocaine • Detroit Rock City • Hallelujah • (I Can't Get No) Satisfaction • Oh, Pretty Woman • Pride and Joy • Seven Nation Army • Should I Stay or Should I Go • Smells like Teen Spirit • Smoke on the Water • When I Come Around • You Really Got Me • and more.
00131159 ....$15.99

First 50 Songs by the Beatles You
Should Play on Guitar

All You Need Is Love • Blackbird • Come Together • Eleanor Rigby • Hey Jude • I Want to Hold Your Hand • Let It Be • Ob-La-Di, Ob-La-Da • She Loves You • Twist and Shout • Yellow Submarine • Yesterday • and more.
00295323..$19.99

First 50 Songs
You Should Fingerpick on Guitar

Annie's Song • Blackbird • The Boxer • Classical Gas • Dust in the Wind • Fire and Rain • Greensleeves • Road Trippin' • Shape of My Heart • Tears in Heaven • Time in a Bottle • Vincent (Starry Starry Night) • and more.
00149269..$16.99

First 50 Songs You Should
Play on 12-String Guitar

California Dreamin' • Closer to the Heart • Free Fallin' • Give a Little Bit • Hotel California • Leaving on a Jet Plane • Life by the Drop • Over the Hills and Far Away • Solsbury Hill • Space Oddity • Wish You Were Here • You Wear It Well • and more.
00287559..$15.99

First 50 Songs You Should Play on
Acoustic Guitar

Against the Wind • Boulevard of Broken Dreams • Champagne Supernova • Every Rose Has Its Thorn • Fast Car • Free Fallin' • Layla • Let Her Go • Mean • One • Ring of Fire • Signs • Stairway to Heaven • Trouble • Wagon Wheel • Yellow • Yesterday • and more.
00131209 ....$16.99

First 50 Songs
You Should Play on Bass

Blister in the Sun • I Got You (I Feel Good) • Livin' on a Prayer • Low Rider • Money • Monkey Wrench • My Generation • Roxanne • Should I Stay or Should I Go • Uptown Funk • What's Going On • With or Without You • Yellow • and more.
00149189 ....$16.99

First 50 Songs
You Should Play on Solo Guitar

Africa • All of Me • Blue Skies • California Dreamin' • Change the World • Crazy • Dream a Little Dream of Me • Every Breath You Take • Hallelujah • Wonderful Tonight • Yesterday • You Raise Me Up • Your Song • and more.
00288843 ....$17.99

First 50 Songs
You Should Strum on Guitar

American Pie • Blowin' in the Wind • Daughter • Hey, Soul Sister • Home • I Will Wait • Losing My Religion • Mrs. Robinson • No Woman No Cry • Peaceful Easy Feeling • Rocky Mountain High • Sweet Caroline • Teardrops on My Guitar • Wonderful Tonight • and more.
00148996 Guitar $16.99

HAL•LEONARD®
www.halleonard.com

Prices, contents and availability subject to change without notice.